The Fine Art of Cabinetmaking

James K

Sterling Publishing

New York

10 9 8 7 6 5 4 3 2 1

Published 2004 by Sterling Publishing Co., Inc.
387 Park Avenue South, New York, NY 10016
Originally published by Van Nostrand Reinhold Company
© 1977, 1992 by James Krenov
Distributed in Canada by Sterling Publishing
c/o Canadian Manda Group, One Atlantic Avenue, Suite 105
Toronto, Ontario, Canada M6K 3E7
Distributed in Great Britain by Chrysalis Books
64 Brewery Road, London N7 9NT, England
Distributed in Australia by Capricorn Link (Australia) Pty. Ltd.
P.O. Box 704, Windsor, NSW 2756, Australia

Printed in China

Sterling ISBN 1-4027-1416-5 $17.95

CONTENTS

The mark of man is the refinement of the hand in action. . . .

Jacob Bronowski
The Ascent of Man

FOREWORD

My first book, *A Cabinetmaker's Notebook*, was, in a sense, a confession of failure. It was about a craftsman trying to live and work in a way that gave him an inner satisfaction, reflecting an almost outmoded, romantic relationship to his craft. The response came as a heartwarming surprise. "You've told us the why," readers wrote. "Now give us some of the how." And so I had the chance to share some more. The books that followed—and our school here in California—seem to have brought encouragement to many craftsmen who had been intimidated by the pressures of professionalism, more and fancier machines, dependence on trends, "art," and the marketplace.

Many of us suspect that wood holds friendly mysteries. It does. And if we are patient and observing and work with wood on an intimate basis, then there are special, personal satisfactions to be discovered. Time-tried tools and methods can be refined, old skills re-learned and put to new use. None of this is to my credit. I have no precious secrets to share. Nor is there a need to re-invent cabinetmaking. People like the Barnsleys in England, Wharton Esherick in America, Peder Maàs in Denmark, remind us of the integrity that has been and should be an inherent part of our craft. For those of us who care enough, cabinetmaking can be an adventure that results in the quiet satisfaction of making objects that will endure and serve their purpose well, bringing pleasures to those who choose to live with them. "Good design," a friend once wrote, "should include the process of doing."

These pages, now, are about doing—about what happens when we do cabinetmaking a certain way and what might happen if we do it another way, or still another. Granted, without a warm and open attitude to our craft, information is of little value; it can even be an index of indifference. It is what we do with what we know that matters, finally—not only the results, but the doing itself. When we discover what wonderful things our eyes and hands are as they seek fine lines and use sharp tools, when we listen to wood and not just use it, then cabinetmaking can take on a new meaning.

—*James Krenov*
1992

INTRODUCTION

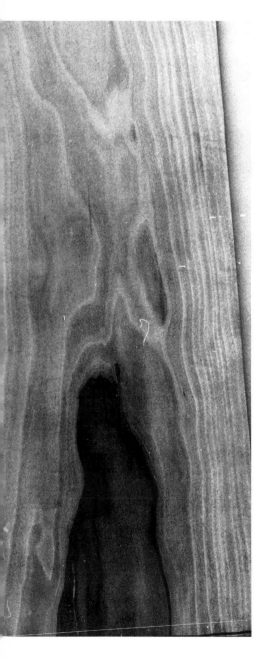

Perhaps it's as well to start by saying this: Without a certain attitude to our craft, information itself is of little value. It is what we do with what we know that matters, finally: not only the results but also the doing itself. After all, that is what we are left with, after the piece is done and has found its owner and we are back working again. What some of us find is an enjoyment we can't weigh against money, recognition, or artistic aura. By whatever term others call it, it is the feeling of doing something we want to do—and doing it well, by measures both honest and sensitive.

These pages are largely about doing—about what happens when we do cabinetmaking a certain way, and what might happen if we do it another way, or still another.

This book is not intended for professional cabinetmakers. It is for amateurs in the true sense of the word: those who love the material and the work of their craft more than anything else about it. And, one should add, who have a fair idea of how demanding wood can be.

Very few persons become cabinetmakers or woodworkers because of the money in it—the housepainter and plumber make more. It's liking to do the work that counts for most of us. Probably it's the wood—whatever each of us means by that statement. Sometimes what it means at the start is not what it turns out to be later on. We begin with the romance, the smells and the feel of wood and tools, the environment of crafts, the workshop—and we meet all too soon wood as a science. We become professionals, not merely by definition but even more so by our attitude, part of which goes back to an efficiency-based training. Subtly, often unnoticed, it turns us aside from the painstaking and dedicated side of our craft to the shortcuts and what I'd call "engineer art." On the way to conventional efficiency we often neglect some emotions and miss some joys. We drift into competition. Less romance, more reality. Less time for those little discoveries, for following them through to their enjoyable and rewarding end, for being at ease.

We're caught. Unless of course one tires of competing that way—speed, originality, design, marketing—and begins to wonder about efficiency. What does it mean, when the chap up the street knows the same tricks, has the same equipment, sees the same shows, reads the same magazines?

Is wood just wood: color and hardness, supply and demand? Why are some tools better, more satisfying to use than others? As to the work itself—there are things one does, and likes to do, that cannot be explained by efficiency. Are these enjoyable moments gained at the price of efficiency—or is there a common sense and a feeling in our odd ways that is more rational than any efficient engineering?

I am not recommending being content with nostalgic oversimplification—subconsciously imitating or borrowing from these—but rather trying to combine unpretentiousness with a seeking of one's own sensitivity. For each level of work there should be the level of doing that work well.

People are different and have different aims. But if there is a common denominator among us, let's hope it is enjoyment of our work—the surprises and the final warmth of it. The road to that shared feeling is a series of small steps. We cross a threshold—and then one small discovery leads to another. Wood is a rich, sensuous material. One can do the most exquisite and refined things with it. Or hack out impulsive, naive messages. Work hours, days, months on one single object. Or sit and carve a toy, a whistle, anything or nothing. Just make shavings. Make pine shavings with a sharp knife, and then run your hand over the bit that is left; feel it, smell it, and think about something you would like to make out of pine. It's nice wood. And not all that easy to work. Really, it is more difficult to make fine crisp joints and smooth shimmering surfaces of pine than some harder wood. Try. With very sharp tools and a light touch.

That's what it's about: being curious, and trying, moving towards the kind of work that is your very own—no matter where you learned it.

1. WOOD

Looking for a way to describe our amateur's relationship to wood, two words come to my mind: one is *curiosity*, the other is *chance*. You live in some particular place—let us suppose it is in a small town. There is a local lumberyard with a few stacks of common woods, the usual thing—fir, oak, butternut, maple, a bit of walnut, some pine. The piece you're apt to end up with has been haphazardly sawn and indifferently stored. Only sometimes in out-of-the-way places you will find just those people who do care, and are friendly, and will take the time to help you find what you want. These persons really care about wood, though with this reservation: they are in business. Seven customers a day like myself and they'll go broke.

At any rate, because there are just a few kinds of wood available, you start looking through the piles to find the best in each, becoming aware of the difference between one plank and another: you just have to. The limited selection can be of indirect help: not having access to infinite supplies of wood prompts you to become more aware of what is there around you.

Curiosity is a start. If the meager supply at the yard discourages you because you have heard about so many different kinds of great wood, it is a good sign. You are caring about wood, have a stubborn interest in it. This curiosity (or whatever you choose to call it) may prove to be of crucial importance. It just might lead you to stumble across the few best pieces in those seemingly uninspiring piles.

Or it may cause you to notice a cut-down apple or pear or elm tree someplace—or the trunk of a tree, or even a stump on the property of someone who may allow you to buy or take this piece of wood. Just think of all the fruit trees that are felled every year in parts of any country. Maybe one at a time, or sometimes even dozens of them at a time in an orchard, cut and piled up to rot or be burned. Fruitwood is often very beautiful, firm in texture, rich with varying colors—it works smoothly and gives fine surfaces. As a rule, fruit trees aren't large. Some cherry and pearwood in Central Europe produces wide clear planks. But fruitwood as most of us imagine and experience it—the wood from local orchards or one's own lot—is usually smaller trees. Small, but not light: it's hard work making such wood usable.

Supposing the log is one foot in diameter and four or five feet long, not too crooked or knotty: you can probably split it into halves or quarters. No use me trying to say which: it depends on the kind of wood, on whether it is very green and wet, or part of a dead tree—on things you will in time be able to judge. Perhaps splitting into quarters is safest to start with; though more work, it will result in less cracking as the pieces dry. But first: peel off most of the bark. Then split the log, which means having to get an axe and a maul and some wedges. If you can, work on the spot—a freshly fallen log even of this size is heavy. Save your back, you'll need it later on.

When you are able to move the wood, you must find a place to store it that is not too dry. Keep it in the air outside at first,

The same pearwood cut to thickness and book-matched reveals subtle patterns and soft colors from reddish to mauve and almost ivory.

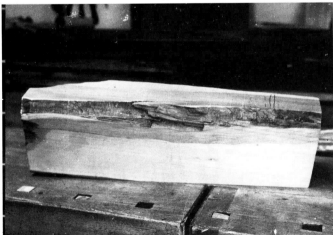

Pearwood. Split into quarters when green, and air-dried slowly. Here rough-trimmed on bandsaw.

Applewood left unopened and stored in unheated garage. Note twist in split: this adds to waste of otherwise fine wood.

under a rain shelter, in a barn or an unheated garage. Wherever stored, the wood will crack some. All kinds of worries go with it—one being that after this first period, about a year of drying, you will need another and less humid space.

Is the wood worth all this effort and more to come? If you have been enthusiastic about it from the start you may find it so. What you save will be fine wood, the kind you'll want to work with and enjoy. Small logs—planks or pieces, which sometimes are smaller than we'd like. Splitting is in itself a limitation.

Recently I have noticed craftsmen tending to obtain wood by sawing it themselves. A concept new in America is emerging: that of the flitch-cut log and fine, thick planks which will later be re-sawn to sizes needed.

A sensible investment for craftsmen who feel like this is a so-called portable mill: a motor-sawmill (some even have two motors) with a special guide-roller attachment. There are several makes available, one in particular very reliable, and such a mill will probably pay for itself within a few months if you use it properly and are ambitious enough. This is easiest if you live outside the concrete jungle, but even from the city, you can easily reach areas where logs are available.

Once you get to where the wood is, and start cutting, you need a lot of energy. You'll need help too, friends willing to participate in this kind of work—and maybe a truck. It can be great fun, like a picnic; you're out all day in the weather, the greenness all round you, working together. Oh, yes; the noise of the saw, the smell of gasoline and the risks of the work itself are there too—but these are in the price of admission. Actually, the final price is not too high: you will be able to obtain some wood which is not available in any lumberyard—at least not yet—and which is more interesting and more personal to you than any counterpart you might find elsewhere. If you are lucky you may find fine wood just for *you*—which may mean anything from an old dry stump of spalted maple to a nice, clear log of ash with a brownish heart. A whole log, maybe two feet in diameter and twenty feet long, can be cut into good sturdy planks in a few hours when the work is properly planned and carried through. A few such logs will pay for your motor-sawmill if you have chosen the right trees. There are, however, many surprises and some disappointments involved in obtaining wood this way.

Portable chain-saw mill with two motors can take logs up to three feet in diameter. Planks can be cut straight and to even thickness from ½ inch and upward.

Portable mill with single motor is
easily handled by one man. The saws
shown here can be obtained from
Robert Sperber, North Caldwell, New
Jersey.

The saws in use.

Often the hardest part of obtaining wood is getting permission to cut the log. There are rules and regulations, local agencies involved, various distant persons, and you have to be diplomatic and clever and perseverant to get at some of the wood which seems so obviously available—until you run into statutes, and people who don't quite understand.

It takes a bit of tact, energy, and patience.

Remember that with any wood you find in the form of logs you must be extra patient: getting it to the state of usability entails labor, time, and space. A consolation: you are apt to obtain a considerable quantity cheaply this way, and once you have the first batch dry, you need only to keep replacing whatever is used. This is the start of a process of rotation where the first stages are very frustrating. Two years go by, and all the wood you have gathered is drying—but not dry.

But once the first batch is properly dried and you start using—and replacing—it, *then* you can slow down your hunt, and be content with a new log only now and then, as the need arises; to keep an "overlap." You always have some dry wood, some nearly ready for use, and some more that is only recently cut.

Once the log is sawn, you are faced with the question of how and where to store it. There is not only romance and adventure in this approach, but also many practical problems. It is not as if you could simply go out and get wood and start working it—that is a trap into which some of us still do fall. With the wood sawn you are only at the beginning of the road that leads to the final usage of it. You have now to stack it properly with air space between the planks. Use sticks about 3/4 or one inch thick as spacers, place them a bit in from the ends of your planks, with maybe three such sticks to a ten-foot length. Protect the ends of the planks with a thick coat of glue, paint, or paraffin to slow down the access of air and minimize splitting. Be sure the wood gets plenty of air: don't put a plastic cover directly over the stack! Resist the temptation to store the wood where it is just a little drier. Keep it in something like outdoor humidity at first. It is so easy to make a foolish mistake that will ruin it.

There is a pile of promising wood in that shed, and you are eager and interested and happy having it—and now you have to let it sit for a year or more. I suppose we enthusiasts cannot accept that. We will keep remembering our wood. We'll go out to the stack, turn over a plank or two, and look at those pieces again, see if there are cracks, discover new areas of color, notice warpage and how the wood is behaving, try to guess just how dry it is—and wish it were drier still. As we do this, our thoughts will begin to turn, ideas will come to us as we think of those patterns, colors, dimensions. We may even go and split off a small piece and carve or plane it a bit—just to get the feel . . . and keep it somewhere in our shop to remind us of this wood we will have in a year or so.

Split or saw or simply buy, it is a never-ending process. Whether you start from the green wood (log) and go through long years of waiting or obtain your wood from companies where the methods of drying and storage bring other uncertainties and frustrations—whatever your source of supply, you must be patient with wood if you really care about it.

Craftsmen forever talk about dry wood: to do good, lasting cabinetwork you need dry wood. Well, dry wood is a myth, or almost a myth. This fact is the cause of disappointments and many small disasters. And though we really do (or should) know better, we still make the mistake of presuming that a given wood is dry; time and again our eagerness to get at the work, our lack of patience with wood, is very difficult to overcome.

Kiln-dried wood may or may not be dry—to assume that it is dry is to court trouble. Everything depends upon how it has been dried in the kiln, and how it has been handled and stored. When it comes out of the kiln it is to all apparent purposes dry, yes. But how many of us actually buy wood during the first few days after it has left the kiln? We go to the yard and select some wood, and buy it, having been assured that it is kiln-dried. We do not ask: kiln-dried *when*? Perhaps months earlier. Since

Wood sawn with portable mill pinned and stacked to air-dry. It should be protected from rain, etc. but given free circulation of air.

Air-dried wood brought into the workshop will be stored here for a year or more before being re-sawn at the start of making a certain piece.

then it has been in the storage sheds (open most of the day to outside air) in humidity that is *not* what it will be in a proper workshop or home.

During the time of storage the process of drying has been partly reversed; moisture has begun to creep into the wood all round—so now the wood is drier inside than it is on the outside. It is no longer evenly dry; tension is building up between the different areas of the wood. This is a source of potential trouble for us. Besides, kiln-dried wood contains other tensions which come from the unnaturally rapid process of drying.

In a book on woodworking an English cabinetmaker says there is no essential difference between air-dried wood and wood that has been dried in a kiln. I find such a statement rather sad. Not because it is untrue—but rather because it has become true for so many cabinetmakers.

Can it be that we are forgetting the feel of air-dried wood under our tools, and no longer notice how the kiln-dried wood is less alive, even in shavings? It actually sounds different—listen as you work.

And the colors: notice that a kiln-dried Italian walnut hasn't the clarity it had before, the soft tints of pink and gray are gone. After all, kiln-dried wood has been steamed, almost cooked. By that forced process some of the elusive chemistry of color has been altered. Sad, if we do not respond to these differences in a material so close to us, so meaningful to our slightest touch and glance.

Somebody says: There shouldn't be any difference; not if the kiln is working right, drying the wood slowly enough. But does the kiln work "right" in these time-is-money times?

Maybe there is no longer any practical difference between natural and synthetic colors in textiles, either—I don't know. But if I were working with textiles I would try to show in my work that there *is* a difference. Just as for me there is a difference between synthetic fibers and wool, the feel of wool against the skin.

If this approach seems old-fashioned, it is, I hope, at least consistent. Some people find my entire attitude unrealistic. Others remark that it is simply romantic. It's all a matter of how we feel. Perhaps, too, of whether we want to go on believing in, and defending what we feel—even when it can't be proved.

The first supplies of wood available to you may affect your work basically: you are apt to adapt what you do to the wood you obtain. If what you can get are mostly small pieces, fruit-wood, odds and ends, you may find yourself doing smallish work. Perhaps, too, you have a rather small workshop or only a part of the basement—you aren't going to do castle gates in that kind of a shop.

On the other hand, you may be lucky and have plenty of space. You may have a tendency to think big, too, and want to work on that scale. Naturally you then try to find wood in the dimensions and quantities you need to do that kind of work.

Your search may take you far and wide—in fact it *should* take you far and wide, unless you are extremely fortunate and live somewhere with all kinds of fine wood readily available.

We who are going to devote ourselves to wood need an eye for it. And a nose: you should be able to sort of scent where there might be interesting wood. Although a few of us tend to be secretive about such matters, word does get around: friends, colleagues, people talk and there are rumors of someone somewhere, of someplace where a certain fine wood can now and then be obtained.

So you come home with a few planks from here and there. For good reasons you may not want to get involved in sawing your own; the initial costs, labor, and risks are against this—and you become an "ordinary" purchaser of wood. A good rule is to buy as much as you can sensibly afford of any wood that excites you and then, quickly, buy a little bit more. I have often experienced the situation where much of the wood I found somewhere was available just at that particular time. Because I simply could not afford all I wanted then, I liked to think that I could come back and get more—"soon," I'd tell myself. But when I returned the wood was gone: *it* did not wait. Very often that particular wood, that flitch-cut log, those odd planks, were what my heart wanted. Sad. Anything else by comparison later on might be good; yes, almost better, but not quite that wood.

As we work and use our wood,

we learn about our craft. We may also become more ambitious, or perhaps more greedy, with regards to our material. A certain kind of cabinetmaker can never have enough wood, or wood that is fine enough. It is a never-ending search. And unless you've got oil in your back yard—or the forests of the world there—you can go broke buying wood while you are dreaming of all the great things you will do with it.

No matter how we get our wood, whether it is odd planks gathered here and there or logs that we have flitch-cut ourselves, if we work with solid wood we have, or should have, a lot of re-sawing to do. Some woodworkers have an aversion to this; certainly, schools have not encouraged it. Re-sawing takes time, there is a waste of wood, the table-saw is dangerous and the band saw cuts too slowly: we can muster all sorts of reasons against re-sawing. One result of such an attitude, and this is noticeable in the work shown, is to avoid re-sawing; we use the dimensions available and adapt our work to these. The result is often a monotony in the piece, a lack in variation and play between different parts; we miss dimensions used with subtlety and balanced against one another. Avoiding re-sawing can result in work that is unnecessarily awkward. This is a pity. Because re-sawing is rather easy, and when done with forethought it more than justifies the time and effort involved.

The first thing is to obtain a good band saw. This is not to say that you cannot re-saw on the circular saw. However, in my opinion you should not. It is dangerous and unpleasant and it is one of the methods which really does waste wood, making unnecessarily wide cuts. By a good band saw, I mean a sturdy, simple machine. Actually, the less sophistication, the more reliability. A rather old-fashioned band saw with a heavy cast-iron frame and steady wheels and simple guides, sometimes with just Bakelite instead of the more modern wheel-guides, is very good indeed and

My eighteen-inch band saw.

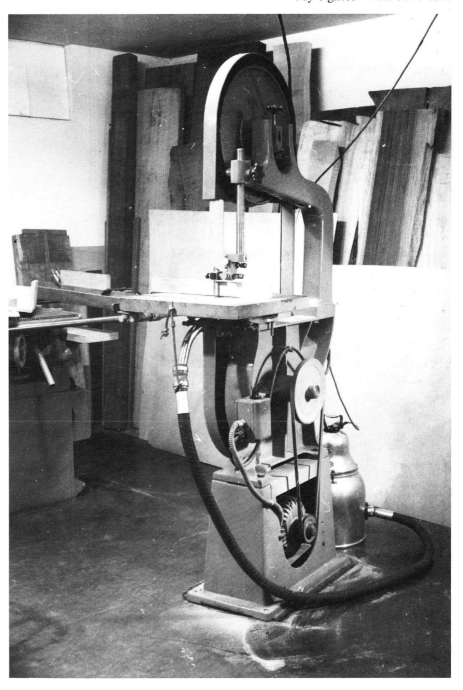

worth buying second-hand, if you can find one. The secret of re-sawing is not a tricky machine. The secret, if any, lies mainly in two things: the blades you use and how you set up your guide for making the cuts.

There are many kinds of band-saw blades, and we will not go into the technical aspects of the different ones. Skip-tooth blades are common and much advertised, but I find the claw-tooth model best for re-sawing wood to average dimensions, including rather thick pieces. The 3/8- and 1/2-inch-wide claw-tooth blades (three teeth to the inch) work very well, both on a smaller saw, perhaps a fourteen-inch one, or a larger band saw, such as a twenty-inch model. Get a few four-tooth-per-inch blades for thinner stock. Form the habit of using only good, sharp blades. In Europe we can have our saw blades, even the hard-edged ones, resharpened. I have about fifty blades, which I use in rotation, they have been sharpened a dozen times or more each. Perhaps once a year I buy five new blades, not more. The resharpened ones, when sharpened right on the machine, are actually sharper than the new ones. And each blade lasts a long time. In America many companies refuse to resharpen hard-edged blades—don't ask me why. It seems a waste to buy, use once, and throw away.

I have had an eighteen-inch band saw for years. It is by far the most important of my machines. Not much for looks, it has done wonderful service steadily. As to the saw-guide, or the

fence, as it is called, usually the one that comes with the saw itself is not very well suited to re-sawing. Not, at least, for rather thick stock. I suggest you make a fence out of two pieces of fairly thick laminate or chip-board (3/4 inch is a good thickness) fitted at right angles, with a block or two to brace them. One is shown in the photograph. You can leave a little space at the overlap down towards the table which will allow the sawdust to come between the stock and the fence there.

One of the main difficulties which occurs is that the relationship between the way the saw-blade wants to cut and the way the fence is set is not correct. We presume that the blade is going to cut straight—that is, at right angles to the table-front and the wheels. But most blades do *not* cut absolutely straight; they tend to drift in one direction or another, usually because the sharpening tools have left a slight burr on the edge of the teeth. Or there may be some other cause, such as the way the saw-wheels are aligned. To check on drift, feed a piece of scrap wood straight along the table, at right angles to the wheels; keep it at that angle and notice whether the blade (cut) drifts in one direction or another. Leave the piece on the table in the same relation the cut has made and then clamp your guide accordingly. Often it will then not be straight across the table, but rather in accordance with the way the blade actually cuts. You set it up that way and clamp it well, perhaps with small blocks

of wood under the saw-table itself. When you feed the work through the saw, remember: do *not* crowd it, feed it slowly and evenly. It does not take much effort, but it does require some patience. Patience in this case, as in so many others, pays off, because the work goes faster than you'd imagine.

If, as you saw, the piece tends to leave the guide, it is because the blade is cutting *in* towards the guide; if you persist in forcing the piece against the guide, the cut will be cupped inward. Conversely, when the guide is set improperly and the cut tends to pull away from the guide, there will be a tendency to cup outward. Either way, the result is a strain on both you and the saw, and a waste of wood.

There is a general tendency to underestimate the worth of a band saw—due, I am convinced, to the stubborn use of the wrong blades, and a disregard for the fine simple facts of re-sawing. (If from the start we don't believe in something, we are less apt to give it a fair chance.) An eighteen-inch band saw will, when properly set up and tuned, cut eight-inch-thick hardwood for hours on end—cut it cleanly and accurately. It will cut six-inch stock right down to a thickness of 1/8 inch suitable for veneer.

Everything has to be right, and kept that way: wheels brushed clean regularly, guides cared for, the blade sharp. And a light but firm hand on the work. If you then push it you lose not only time but also wood, some of which may be irreplaceable. Remember: once things start going

Guide for re-sawing on the bandsaw.

Guide set properly ensures fine, even cut.

Bandsaw blades often "drift," making cuts that are not at right angles to the front edge of the saw-table.

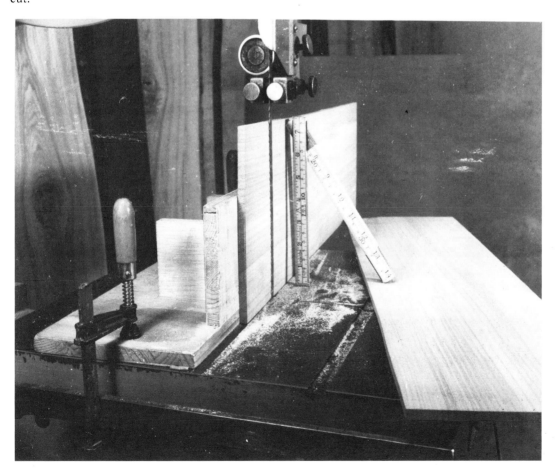

wrong and you become irritated, you are apt to make even more mistakes and spoil even more wood, and then all your plans are upset.

It is very important in our work to keep things going well, so that one does not reach that state of irritation. Then one cannot work well. Even the finest ideas and the best wood and even an initial enthusiasm can't help us once we get bogged down in a lot of small errors that keep accumlating. So at the first sign of difficulty, stop and back up a bit, think not only in terms of detail, but even more in the light of what it is you want to accomplish—and take the time to get on the right track again.

Perhaps I am into this matter of re-sawing a little too soon, though with the facts of this in mind it may be easier to relate some of our ambitions to the wood we have. Certainly, before re-sawing in earnest we need to do a lot of thinking: the more interesting ideas we have about some piece we'd like to make, and the finer our wood, the more careful we need be not to spoil things. If you are too eager, you might cut a plank crosswise at a point you think is right, but you have not laid out the work properly, or re-checked everything—and now it turns out you have cross-cut in the wrong place. That's a mistake almost as irreparable as cutting off a finger.

Looking for wood, and planning one's work in terms of years to come, it is well to keep in mind not only the various good points about any particular wood

but also the troubles that often accompany those qualities.

For instance: there is shavings wood and there is dust wood. Most species of wood, especially those of North America and Europe, are shavings wood: when you work them in machines or by hand you get shavings. And the chances are good that with shavings you also get clean-cut shimmering surfaces and burnished edges. The shavings themselves are nice, too; they polish your floor as you sweep up.

Dust woods are another matter. You work with doussie—a good wood otherwise—and ex-

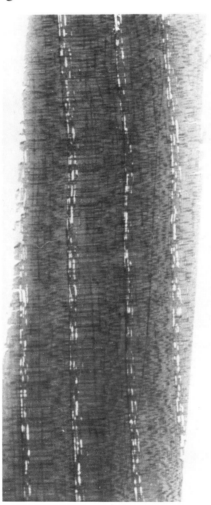

cept for a few crumbs in the machines, the shop is full of thick, heavy, dry dust, lingering in the air for what seems like hours. You cough, you sneeze, you swear. Your nose drips and your eyes water. If you're unlucky you develop an allergic symptom, break out in a rash. Maybe not from doussie, but very likely from mansonia, cocobolo, or rosewood. You sweep the floor three times in quick succession, wipe off the machines, benches—and still everything is dusty.

Another sort of meanness in wood is the crystalline substance in teak, afromosia, and the like—the stuff is similar to what rubs

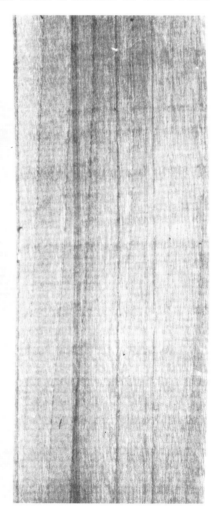

Ash (left) and maple shavings.

off bad sandpaper. It dulls your tools beyond all reason.

To satisfy your curiosity or maybe win a bet, you can work some of this dust wood now and then; it is a good way to find out which of them you dislike most—or dislikes you most.

But in the long run you'll probably have to decide either to get carbide cutters for your machines (very expensive), buy loads of saw-blades (more money), and invest in a good waste-removal system—or to

The crumbs from hand-planed doussie. In machine-working this wood, the crumbs are even smaller.

stick to other kinds of wood.

Yet against this commonsense solution is one's stubborn feeling for the color, the texture, the very weight of a wood like cocobolo. Or the wonderful, wavy pinkish-grayish ripples in Indian laurel. I found some planks of this in London, brought them home. They cost a mint. After two or more years of drying, they were ready to use. I had planned a large cabinet and started to work eagerly. I finished the cabinet, but the dust was like sand, heavy on everything, and almost impossible to sweep up, even with the help of sweeping compound.

I intended to sell, or even give away, the rest of that Indian laurel. Yet somehow I still have it. Maybe, I tell myself in weaker moments, maybe if I make only very small things out of it, one at a time, at long intervals, I could . . . . Ah, well!

A person who uses only small quantities of wood—for whatever reasons—need not have all these worries on a large scale. You may be making puppets, wooden toys, salad spoons; you need not be a cabinetmaker. Whatever our expression, interest in wood is our meeting-point. Earlier, I called it curios-

ity; I mentioned luck. With these you make discoveries. You develop a feel for what is in a log or a plank, you care—and that is a driving force. It is the beginning of an excitment which carries you on to other discoveries, to the heart of the work itself.

At the start this interest or curiosity is more a matter of feeling than of accurate facts. Finally it is both feeling and facts, but of the two, feeling is the more important. Without curiosity and a sense leading to the living richness that is in some woods, one will always remain something of an engineer—even as a successful craftsman. Many successful craftsmen are, alas, only engineers.

Wood is elusive in its patterns, changing in its moods, and only partly predictable in its ways. What is vital in all this is to build up your experience on the basis of what I would like to imagine are the natural laws of wood—all the while allowing your sense of curiosity and enthusiasm for this wonderful material to help you put together the intimate experiences that make cabinetmaking something more —or is it less?—than a profession.

I suppose the first stages of becoming a craftsman are very, very important; it is then we go through hardly recognizable critical periods. Times when, often by chance, we make discoveries that increase our interest and enthusiasm and give us strength. This helps us further; we are able to overcome disappointments, and go on. We are vulnerable: the remark of a teacher, a word from a friend can make a difference in our lives. If we do not come upon those discoveries, and use them, then we may not reach the point where we can, with this first knowledge and early eagerness, be rewarded by the joyous harmony of wholeness in our work.

Unidentified Brazilian hardwood sent to author. Planks contained streaks and whorls of brown and tan. The wood cracked, warped, almost refused to dry.

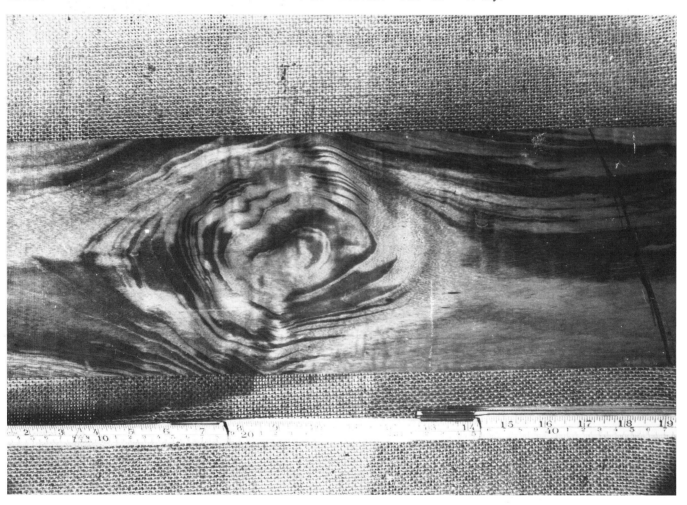

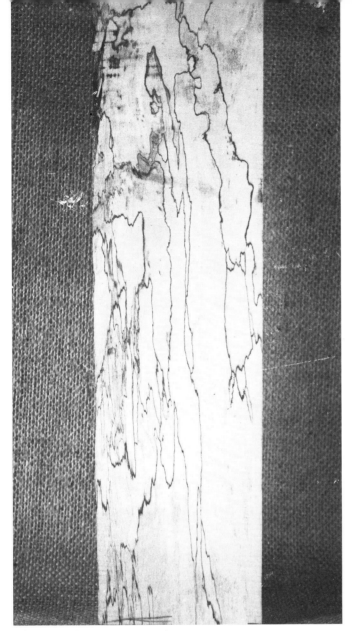

Boxwood. From a small billet found in London. It had been stored outdoors, and is spalted. There were many cracks and much waste.

Cocobolo. A billet, opened, revealed extensive damage. However, the usable wood was a joy.

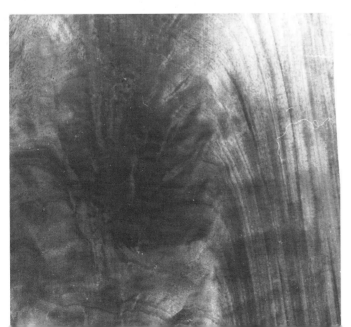

Mahogany pyramid, solid wood, cut about twenty-five years ago. There are subtle, fernlike pattern traces along the middle area.

You have to reach a point where small revelations and adventures show you the way, and you say to yourself: "Ah, so *that's* what it's about. Now I see; this is interesting. This is something I can use!" It may be the challenge of a piece of fine wood, a knife that fits your hand, a plane with which you will enjoy working. But if some of the questions and the answers come from the wood itself, I think that is a good sign.

When you do not have exciting wood, or simply have not enough different kinds of wood, it is easy—a bit too easy, really—to make excuses for the way you work and blame it on the simple wood. We should be able to work well with the wood we have while hoping for the wood we'd like to get.

I used to be very absorbed by unusual and "fine" woods, and spent far too much time running about looking for these, searching for the inspiration of ever more striking colors and patterns. This is all right, but it can be a diversion. Now, after many years, I am rediscovering some of the simpler woods. Soft and rather commonplace woods such as pine and fir and cedar make their own demands on the cabinetmaker. A general attitude is that one makes chests out of these, clumsy boxes, floors,

houses: they are seldom associated with *delicate* work.

Such prejudices are an easy way of getting around the challenge of refinement. It can be enlightening to make a well-balanced, very small pine box with delicate joints, let us say a box for a teabowl or some other little ceramic piece. Actually it takes more skill, sharper tools

and greater patience than it would using some harder and more "suitable" wood.

Imagine an exercise where we are asked to make small boxes, for example, out of three or four simple woods like pine and oak and maple—boxes with the same dimensions, the same spacing and size of joints in each. We will then look at these objects, and

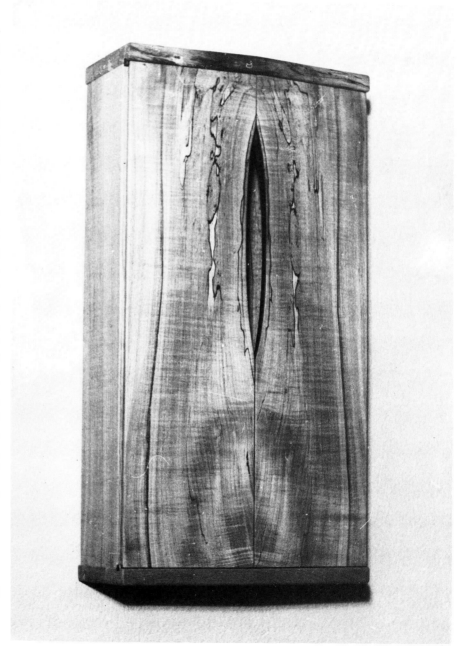

Cabinet of spalted maple. The wood was sawn with a portable mill at Rochester, New York, in 1973, the cabinet made in Stockholm three years later. The odd opening between the doors is the result of using the shape along an outer edge of the plank.

22

talk about them and notice—as we did or did not notice during the work itself—how differently these woods react to the tools and methods we have used. How in one wood the joints were easier to make and in another they were more difficult: some woods tear and chip while others are more firm; some are resilient and the joints press one half into the other, while with wood that is more dense and brittle the joints do not go together unless every dovetail is right on—as if we were working with stone.

We compare these boxes, and though they are alike in size and detail, our experiences of having made them are quite different.

Then another exercise: each of us is allowed to make our own versions of the preceding boxes, out of the same woods, but now choosing the proportions and the joints according to what we sense each wood calls for. Unless we feel intimidated (which we sometimes do in schools), we will make our boxes as we want to make them. More or less in close relation to the wood, and the purpose of the box, and our judgment as to how all this should be.

Instead of being alike, the boxes will be only similar.

In maple the joints will somehow have become more finely tapered and differently spaced than in pine or oak. If we are consistent, even the proportions—the way we do the details of the lid, or of the bottom, or how we finish the corners—will be different, too. The oak, if it gets what it asks for, will have a heavier air about it. With each wood there should emerge a separate and distinct box.

This very simple work teaches us that *the same object, when made in the same way but out of different woods, will seldom look right or feel right in more than one of these woods. If done in accordance with each wood and one's own sense of workmanship, both the experience of the work and the result will be different each time.*

The scale of what we do, despite what some say, is not decisive for its message. We don't *have* to impress people with the size or scope of our work. The simplest little object can contain all our knowledge and skill. Our relationship to wood rests on how we use it. The number of basic joints in cabinetmaking does not exceed five—all the others are an extension of these. The fundamental constructions we use can be counted on our fingers—yet the truly personal expressions of these are infinite.

The realization of this can make one feel humble. The knowledge that wood cannot be pushed around, so to speak, that it doesn't want to be forced—is sobering for some of us. Wood is a live material, with a will and integrity of its own. It can split, break, bend, buckle, and shrink —all within the boundaries we enforce upon it. That is why it sooner or later reveals whether or not we have listened to it, and cared.

Listening is a search. It can lead us to the refinement of the violins. Or to the popular exaggeration of the drums. It depends upon what we are (and want). Of these two paths, refinement is the more elusive. Those times when we achieve a sensitive and harmonious balance in our work are the finest because they are so dearly earned.

We are apt to take for granted or ignore work that is unimpressive: most people will shrug at a low-tone approach. But a few do see in it a relief from the pressure of originality. A calmness that is a sort of new confidence separating one from the competition of efficiency. For some craftsmen it is not defeat. Humility is not the same as being humiliated, though at times we experience it as such.

From the simplest object we move on. We are aware that wood is something more than just a submissive material. And if we are sensitive, then we develop our feelings to include a sense of method, the logic of how we put things together. Cabinetmaking is a complex craft, and it may seem frightening at first not to know the principles of construction, the uses of machines, or the fine points of certain tools. Ours is a constant search for a language of our own. Knowledge is available, and the details of technical skill, equipment, and specific materials are problems each of us will overcome in his or her own way. I can only make suggestions and share a few personal experiences.

But if we are not to become simply professional woodworkers involved in and shaped by the mold in which professionalism would have us, we must guard our enthusiasm as we would our life. Long after we know a great deal, we must preserve that enthusiasm.

The facts and knowledge of centuries of woodworking are available to us. Yet it is difficult to imagine any book, or books, that will give us a true sense of the flexibility with which this experience can be used by us, the way we can make common knowledge our own and with the help of it express something personal. By "personal" I mean more than a visual experience, more than form or design. It's our final mark I have in mind—the craftsman's fingerprints on the work. Do they show?

To say that dovetails are handmade joints is to say nothing. To tell about dovetails in terms of angles and the traditional regular spacing is a bit more—but dull. To *give a feeling* of this classic joint in various situations—how spacing can be made less monotonous and at the same time more logical, how dovetail angles are related to different woods and the sense of tension in each, to convey the rhythm of a joint and its clarity of purpose—is something else again.

We need that kind of looking at our work, for better or for worse. In the long run it is what keeps some of us going. That and our love for wood.

During visits to North America I have often wondered why relatively few exotic woods can be had there. Even some of what might be called classic cabinetmakers' woods are hard to find, and the little that is available is very expensive. One can sometimes order selected tropical wood from the country of origin —or even through a European dealer—at a cost equal to or less than the wood specialty yards charge. The limited supply of some fine cabinetmakers' woods is, I suppose, partly due to their no longer being available in quantity: they are slow-growing, they have been harvested without thought for the future, many species are almost extinct. Who has used so much of these rare woods? *We* have. All of us have taken part in this waste that is called veneer. Whether through ignorance or bad taste, we all support the quasi-wood craze, the square miles of veneered executive paneling, the offices, corridors, washrooms lined with it. The finest logs of almost any harvested wood go to the veneer factories.

How much expensive junk has been manufactured out of rosewood! From a few sleek custommade Danish chairs we get a spreading disease of pretentious nonsense. French and Italian walnut at its best is princely wood; mild, elegant, wanting to be made into refined things. It too is almost gone now—the finest has been more or less wasted on veneer and reproduction work, "period" furniture.

Beautiful woods have been literally hunted to death, like birds and animals we do not understand and in our ignorance must pursue and kill. Think of a fine wood like English brown oak, and the way it has been popularized these last ten years, made a mode for architects and designers, become expensive beyond reason, ruthlessly cut and dried—pushed—until now the best of it is gone.

And gone, or going, too, are some of the traditional cabinetmakers' woods. This is not so surprising as it is sad: they represent not luxury but richness—the wealth of expression that belongs to our craft. I think it is a pity we do not encourage suppliers to stock these woods, include them in the experiences of education so they could stimulate a certain kind of student in a special and positive way.

So much wood is being wasted, misused, ignored; it would be only right if some of us who care could be given the chance to work well with many different woods —including tropical ones—and in turn remind people of the pleasure they can bring. After all, we use only a tiniest fraction of what is available—if one could but obtain it.

A part of our frustration is geographic, another economic. Some, too, is laziness; we are not curious enough, we don't ask for some of these fine woods, or encourage others to do so. In a group, we might get results.

As woods become remote and scarce, a commonsense working knowledge of them is harder to come by. When and if we find a rare tropic wood we don't always know how to handle it without humidity tables and measuring instruments and misleading advice. We have to develop a sense, almost an instinct. It doesn't come easily—these dense, heavy woods *are* difficult to get along with. They often have a fascination of their own; weight, color, texture are strange and elusive to us. But along with the attraction

24

come doubts: it is very difficult to know where you stand in regards to working such wood. There is little of it available. When you find it, nobody seems to really know enough about it. Where has it dried, and how? Where has it been stored, for how long? Is it a porous wood like doussie which, though it is heavy, dries fairly well? Secupira is similar in structure; one can imagine the air will creep in among those coarse fibers, too: but no—secupira will crack apart in the same storage where doussie survives.

You find something promising. Having been told it is "dry," you take it from a warehouse in Brooklyn or San Francisco or New Orleans and bring it to your shop. Even when you know that "dry" can mean different things to different people, the temptation to get at the wood is almost irresistible. So you bring it in. And after a few days you hear a pl-i-ing as it starts to crack. A sound that echoes in the pit of your stomach, it is a desperate feeling to hear and see those cracks develop. You move the wood to cooler and more humid air, wondering: for how long? What's with this tropical wood, anyway, was it *that* wet?

I found a pile of old stock in a yard not far from Stockholm in 1963, when the last of the wood once kept for the old-fashioned kind of cabinetmaker was nearly gone, as was the need to carry any more such wood: the yard was being cleaned up and re-equipped to meet new times. There were these grimy planks, some of them thirty years and more old, and the gnarled little foreman grinned,

Three-inch plank of tropic hardwood. Kiln dried, then stored in the workshop for four years. When a length was removed, the wood checked at the opened ends.

Tropical wood, kiln dried—typical short, deep checks follow grain swirls and "local" strains.

pleased, when I showed my interest. No, he did not know offhand all the kinds of wood they had thrown in the corner; there was some afromosia and ubata teak and karri-wood and . . . those two big planks? Probably incensio. Incensio? I asked. Yeah. African, he said. We chipped off a piece, it split easily, and he sniffed the grayish orange wood and handed it to me. Yeah, that's it—incensio. The word sounded of smell. And sure enough the wood gave off an odd, pungent aroma I was supposed to recognize. Ye-es, I nodded, trying not to reveal my ignorance. Though neither I nor you will find the name incensio in a list of woods, here it was, with its strange smell and local name which is perhaps used in some remote jungle place. But I would not find it here again. After these planks, we wouldn't even know how to ask for such wood; where to ask, or whom.

A name, a smell, a rich color. The planks were over three inches thick, fifteen inches or so wide, maybe twenty feet long, and unbelievably heavy; I could not even budge, let alone lift one end.

We agreed on a clearing-out price; a guess on their part since they had no record of purchase or source, and nobody could remember what the wood originally cost. It didn't really matter: I wanted this incensio and I am a fool when it comes to wood. If I find something I want, I have to have it, cost what it may. If the wood is fine, its cost as a material is not so important to me as what to do with it. In other words, with fine wood I am en-

couraged to do good work—and if the work is good someone will pay a fair price for it, and everything will balance without anyone being hurt. (If a piece that is otherwise fine has a section full of faults, I often saw this off and leave it at the yard to be given away. My shop is so small I have no room for any wood that I cannot use.)

The foreman cross-cut the two incensio pieces so I could at least move them around and into my shop. A week or so went by, and then this wood started to crack. I had treated the ends and a bit in from these, put the wood in the coolest part of the shop, on the floor. Nothing helped; the wood kept cracking. I am used to tropical wood checking a little as it dries—small short checks at the ends and even on the surfaces, but not deep, and with the wood settling down after this, causing no more trouble. Mostly it is like that.

My incensio, however, did not check—it split! Twang! Long, mean cracks that appeared almost over night, and kept growing. Of course I moved the wood outside. I let it rest for a year under the porch, brought it in—and it kept on popping. It had already been "drying" for twenty years or so, what was one year more or less?

I did the only thing left to do—I sawed the four big pieces into smaller thickness and widths (it took some doing) to be used one day for smallish things—if the wood did not fall apart. Cut in small dimensions, it sort of gave up the fight, and relaxed. I made a jewelry box or two of it, a small

table, some drawers in cabinets of other woods.

Some of these tropical woods are so terribly dense that the air simply does not get inside fast enough or-evenly enough for the wood to dry without checking badly. "Ordinary" wood, even our more common hardwoods, that have been seasoned for a year or two are ready to be brought indoors for final drying. Not so these densest of tropical woods. Even if they were once kiln dried and then stored somewhere waiting for an odd buyer, when we do find them they are apt to be neither dry nor wet, but at a stage I'd call simply unready. They are too dense, too slow, too full of interwinding fibers and local tensions to stand the change from usual commercial storage to the climate of a cabinetmaker's workshop. Take it slower, allow for intermediate stages, a half-dry place, and then drier. Yes, I know. But *however you handle this wood, it is desperately slow drying.* Whether it is lignum vitae, ebony, box, lemon, or tulip, you have to be patient with it. And in order to be patient enough—which is very, very patient—you no doubt have to believe in the wood you find, and want, and get.

It isn't worth the bother? Why tell about so much grief? I sometimes wonder. Then I go through some of the wood I have had for years now, uncover the light and the dark secupira and in a far corner, the rippling yellow *perobinha crespa* sent to me from Brazil, a few precious leftovers of spalted boxwood from a small yard by a muddy canal in London

—and I say to myself: There it is. There's what I could save. And it is worth all the effort!

I understand those who do not agree. Though when they go so far as to dismiss tropical woods (as some do) I protest: to me this is not only a prejudice smacking of ignorance, but also a sad limitation. It is comparable to saying that a textile artist should be content with working in cotton or wool or nylon—when we know there are so many other interesting materials: sisal, jute, Thai silk. The difference between hornbeam and English brown oak is comparable to that between jute and Thai silk. One is richly coarse, and the other is most exquisitely silky. You don't think in the same way about the jute as you do about silk; you don't make the same sort of dress or coat or blouse out of the one as of the other. The way you envision a garment, how you then cut and sew it, will depend on what you know and feel about the material. And this is what you gradually develop as you get acquainted with various woods. It isn't the name of a wood. It is not even the hardness or the weight or the smell or the color. It's the *sum total* of all the qualities it contains that gets to you and stays with you, sets you thinking in a particular way, feeling rich and impatient, eager to start working with that piece of that particular wood. I know very well this is an unrealistic and luxurious feeling. I know, too, that there is an infinite variety of temperate and northern woods that are thrilling—and that behave in a more civilized manner. And still I persist; expose myself to the search, the struggle, and the expense—and the reward—of these odd and unpredictable exotic woods. They stir me, I can't help it.

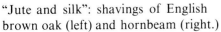
"Jute and silk": shavings of English brown oak (left) and hornbeam (right.)

27

What is "exotic"? Why is cocobolo more exotic than a piece of birds' eye maple with a cut that reveals the wonderful greenish heart and the mauve tones with tiny birds' eyes scattered through these like stars in an evening sky? Or lovely southern pecanwood with its firm knots, and the fragrance lingering around it? These are exotic to some of us—not in the sense of location, much less of local patriotism, but by the measure of actual experience. These are rich woods. I enjoy them, too—in case you suspect I am a tropical wood bug.

Then there are pure curiosities which we share—sometimes boastfully—or even exploit. A table with its leaf of rare wood, impressively polished, the edge rough as the cuts were made, with the bark still on or merely peeled off—such a table, on a stand that's half Danish, half you-name-it, will get by. More: it will sell for good money.

If we use spalted maple it will catch an eager eye, too. And rightly so: certainly some of the softer, we might say "tame" woods are as exciting or even more exciting than their wild Asian or African cousins. With our curiosity and energy we can find bits of these lovely woods almost forgotten in small yards. Maybe we know of a mill out in the sticks somewhere with one or two men sawing local wood for whoever wants it, sawing sorts that are not typical cabinetmakers' woods, and yet sometimes running into something truly beautiful which they put aside "just in case," because they too feel for it. Then you come along. They sense your sincere interest, and nice things happen.

Such surprises occur, too, in the most common of lumberyards; to exclude these places as a source of fine wood is to be unfair not so much to the yard as to the craftsman. Among stacks and stacks of wood that some of us would not even consider using are a few precious planks which nobody has cared about, or even knows are there. Until we find them, and coax someone into picking them out of the pile for us. And then we take them home. They aren't many, these finds, but they help to keep us going, we can make small, special things of them—until we find something better.

Much of this depends upon chance, and personal relationships. Some of us enthusiasts are moody people. Still: we do make friends. I believe there is an affinity among those who care about wood that helps things along.

From the start, try to build up a "play" between the wood and what you want to make. Weave together the things you wish to do with what the wood seems to call for. You have an idea, you've thought it through, even if there is only a rough sketch as yet. (With me there may not even be a sketch—just the wood and an idea, in that order.) Think about the relationship of the various qualities of the wood to the operations involved, and the *meaning* of the work. Will it be hand-cut shapes and surfaces, subtle details—or mostly machined, sanded, a matter of confidently predetermined proportions? Measure this in the light of your idea, the mood of it. Think again, and include an ideal, a guess, a wish.

If this way of going about things is right for you, it will emerge. One day it will be there, as a sort of natural condition; something you feel rather than think about. Well, both, really—though the feeling should be there first. You do a thing a certain way; it feels right—and afterwards you conclude that it *is* right, it's good.

I am not exactly talking about "design." This word comes up, and I must admit I do not like the word! Probably I associate it with cleverness. With *using* ideas, speculating in form and function to entrance a gullible audience. "Designers" draw things instead of making them, I feel. When people say that my work is an example of design (good design, they hasten to add), I, vain fellow, smile happily, and mumble something about "design after, not before. . . ." But a flicker of doubt remains. Does not "design" stand for an enforcement of ideas upon a material? We often choose a predictable, obedient material to carry out our intentions. Professional designers think mostly in terms of multiples, of production. But for me, wood is not predictable, nor obedient. I am against anyone presuming that wood obeys a clever idea. Wood is alive, and not always obedient. But if design is what some of us craftsmen feel and do, and also what most designers think out—then let it be so.

Wood is not just color: mahogany is reddish, oak is brown, maple is yellowish, and so on. Wood is color *and* shadings *and* lines—in all sorts of nuances. These subtleties come and go, and if we are not interested enough, they evade us. Wood does not possess the qualities of hardness or softness by themselves: wood is also resilience and suppleness and brittleness—to be experienced in relation to joints, shapes, surfaces, and edges. These qualities are not only seen, but also actually felt, since much of our best experience of wood is through our fingertips. I notice that many woodworkers tend to leave hard edges in the pieces they produce: some of these remind us of television sets rather than friendly furniture. Because wood, being a material for our hands as well as eyes, wants to be formed into definite and yet pleasant shapes and edges and corners.

Wood grain is not merely lines, but also layers, which can be with us or against us as we work. This is a generalization, because within those lines which we think tell us how the grain runs there are fibers whose direction it is much more difficult to predict. These fibers, like fur on a cat, are only friendly in one direction.

Ordinarily, running a piece over a jointer will tell us which way most of the grain goes; even in rowed wood one direction is often better than the other. More often than not our pieces are less than a flitch-cut width, and do not include both outsides of the log. However, if we do have such

a wide "straight across" plank we should be extra careful: the grain may be different at the two outside edges. This is because trees often twist as they grow, responding mysteriously to the sun and the wind and the seasons. Make trial cuts with a plane or knife before machining such pieces.

Unless you are very careful in working it, wood with uneven grain will cause trouble: you are apt to raise the grain somewhere. To correct this, you will have to make an extra cut or two on the jointer or planer—and there go some of your intended dimensions. So again: allow for surprises, the unpredictable is there among those nice pieces of wood. For a patient person with sensitive fingers it is often possible to feel the direction of the surface fuzz, or fiber-ends—provided the wood is not rowed. Also the practiced eye can detect this "fur"

when the light is good and the wood has been cleaned on a jointer.

This is a good time to mention a simple detail, ridiculously simple, really, and yet overlooked as such details are apt to be: namely, how to keep track of the grain in any number or sequence of pieces coming from the same plank. We make a sloping mark right through the whole edge of the plank—the slope being back "*with* the fur" (grain) in relation to the first part you surfaced. Do this on both edges of the plank, since sooner or later you will work other parts, and if you have marked only one side, it may be among the ones you plane. Then you'll wonder which way to machine a re-sawn piece, and if you are not lucky you might turn it the wrong way. None of us is lucky all the time.

Direction of grain marked on a succession of pieces to be machined.

Grain is full of meaning. It is not simply a direction in which you can plane easily or work easily versus another direction which will raise the wood and cause roughness. Grain is a part of the graphics of wood; it is how we use grain with its tensions and countertensions that gives meaning to shapes and creates shapes within shapes. You may make a rectangular object which appears almost oval because of the way you have turned the pieces and used the grain of the wood; intentionally you give the rectangular shape a soft and friendly appearance. Whereas if you turn the pieces of wood the opposite way, this same rectangle will seem to have exaggerated, sharp corners that are quite repellent to the eye. Similarly there are subtleties of color

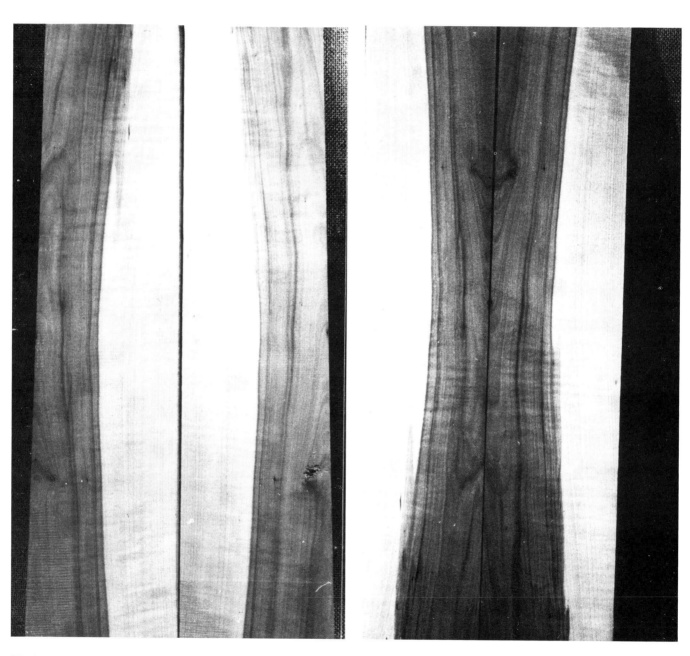

The "hard" and "soft" effects of the same wood resawn and book-matched in two ways. Applewood.

in wood and strange shadings that can make a flat surface seem illusively convex or concave. Shifts of color can give depth to the simplest surface; remember that a convex form, if it is lighter in the middle, will be accentuated, whereas a concave form is at its best when the wood is chosen so there is a darker shading in the middle. These are the ABCs of graphics, and yet, among cabinetmakers and other woodworkers these rules are neglected, often because too much attention is fixed on originality of idea and form. Originality can easily become an end in itself, a limitation: the trees between us and the forest, depriving us of some of the adventure of working with wood.

Top and bottom pieces of frames selected with intention, but not enough care.

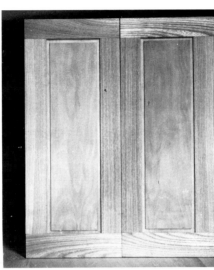

Carelessness—and disharmony.

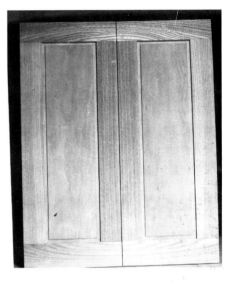

An intended "oval" effect carried through.

With the same pieces as in the "oval" frame: an effect of sharp corners and "outward" sweeps.

Here the grain creates an effect of inward slope, and a "drooping." This might prove an asset with inward sloping doors.

Grain set this way works well with doors set at a slight outward angle, or "V."

31

Within any basic form and many a good idea there is also a quiet richness—if you just turn to the wood for it. This is why, as you become more familiar with wood, all these aspects take on new meaning. You feel richer as you go along. You are not just a cabinetmaker or a woodworker like all the rest. You are an artist—there are all these things you can express with your material.

Cabinet of English brown oak. Pattern of top piece resulted in a uniquely interesting relationship to doors. This was at first a guess—and then luck.

The ability to use grain pattern effectively is one of the qualities distinguishing a fine chair maker from an ordinary one. The way he selects the wood for legs, armrests, and back pieces is then an art. He knows what will happen when you saw a curve from wood with the growth rings in a certain direction. As we saw a shape we can intentionally use the grain pattern to accentuate it.

In the case of table or chair legs and also armrests, it is best to have the rings on a diagonal. If the grain is flat—that is to say parallel to two sides of a leg—then between these two surfaces

and the other two (where the grain is vertical) there will be a great difference of pattern. Such legs may be pleasing when seen from one side—but when do we see them only that way? We see the adjoining side also—and in this case it is very disturbing, with the flat grain in coarse, incoherent patterns.

With armrests and backs—in fact, with most parts of a chair—we can use the grain to add meaning to a shape. This takes some thinking, and at an early stage, too—when we have the plank before us and are laying out the various parts of our chair.

It also reminds us that it is an advantage to have wood flitch-cut, since in any log there are several outside or away-from-center cuts where the grain is at angles such as those we'd like now—if we can only figure out how to lay the pattern.

A way to orient yourself if you become confused and cannot quite visualize how the grain relates to the shape you want is to practice this with scraps of wood which you saw to similar shapes. Make pencil lines corresponding to the grain, and "see where they go," so to speak. In time this will become a habit. Or almost a habit: being in a hurry, anyone can get confused.

One of the simplest ways to observe the reactions of grain to various forms is to make wooden bowls. If you cut into the wood from the side where the grain is on an upward arc, you obtain a series of oval rings or an oval pattern. Cutting from the other side you would achieve the opposite: a curved "hourglass" pattern. Other combinations, with the grain at various slopes to the surface, will only give you lopsided variations of the basic patterns.

This, I am afraid, is beginning to sound like engineering. It's like saying: The message of a good bowl is the sum of the shape and its relationship to the wood pattern.

But is that all?

I know a woodcarver who

Observing the direction of grain (annual rings) and applying it to a desired shape.

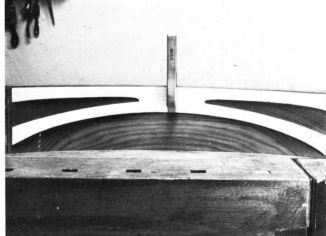

makes bowls and little boxes out of burls. He gets burls, mostly birch, and dries them very carefully. "They are so fragile," he says, protecting them like a basket of fruit from severe changes in temperature or humidity. Then he does this carving, making large or small bowls, depending on what he can get out of each precious burl. He is a truly skilled carver, and the way he cuts that curled and twisted wood is fantastic. So are the brown-speckled lacy patterns. And the finish! He has a workshop full of these bowls, boxes, small trays for cheese, and the like. He doesn't want to part with them. He is a teacher; he does not have to sell his woodwork for his living—except, as he explains, to some nice person who appreciates it. Perhaps one day he will have a modest showing of his work; he isn't sure.

I wonder if people notice that with all the technical skill, love, and care put into them, many of his bowls still lack something? They are not all of them alive.

It is sad, almost tragic.

Somehow the bowls are too perfect, or perhaps it would be more accurate to say they are too rigid. Something—an unevenness of line, a touch of the unpredictable—is lacking. I cannot articulate it: its just that for me something is missing.

Maybe if the wood had been not quite so dry, and had warped a trifle. Ah, but then it might have cracked. What if my friend had been more relaxed when he carved those shapes, so that his intuition could play its part in the work?

Even if you are the kind of craftsman who does rather modest work, who is not brilliant in ideas and techniques, but who works patiently and well, you will use various subtleties of wood. Perhaps you'll use them best, most intuitively, just because you are that patient and cautious type of craftsman. Some subtleties are lost or wasted on wild and wooly shapes where soft shadings and fine details are not so important as *form*. Whereas with more subdued shapes those nuances— what I would call a sculptor's touch—become a part of the expression. Small objects, finely weighed, with pattern in patterns—done by someone with a light touch for whom that particular wood is precious.

It is a pity when the public— and others who judge work in wood—are not enough aware of how much it takes on the part of the craftsman to give us objects that are simple, refined— and interesting as well. Because of ignorance, as well as prejudice, we exclude so much.

We need to see better. To see— in the way that Yanagi meant, which is to sense and notice (in that order) even before we know. That seemingly odd bevel, that uneven curvature of line, the surface flat yet somehow alive— these we see only when we have first sensed the meaning of their conversation.

The craftsman works, looking and looking again, from one revelation to another—often by way of mistakes, listening to the material, coming upon unexpected signals. Good things and

bad things: knots that should not be where they are, fascinating colors that appear as if out of nowhere. It takes effort. But it gives something more in return.

Some wood shows from the beginning that it is bowed and twisted, sprung—some does not. Wide-open cracks can indicate hidden tensions; a plank from the outside of a crooked log is apt to spring, too. Elm and oak are bad in this respect: many of the tropical woods with their rowed fibers and wavy grain are even worse—if that is a consolation.

If we do not discover it earlier, this tension reveals itself as we saw the wood: one half of a piece may bow crazily while the other half remains straight. And you wonder: what will the next cut be like? Wood that springs like this is mean; do not rely on it! If used in large sections, it will continue to make trouble. So if you have other stock, use it. But if you *must* use a sprung plank, make allowances for further spring when you re-saw and machine it.

Warpage is another problem. Hardly any plank is really straight when dried. Whether it is in the kiln or in the open air or protected in your workshop, nearly all wood warps, some more, some less. Besides guessing and hoping, you should observe, and learn as much as possible about your wood: where it came from, how it was dried, the way the grain is—notice everything you can about it. Relate this to what you know about how wood reacts to moisture and to drying.

The strains and stresses of warpage have been described as a series of rubber bands stretched along consecutively wider arcs from a common center—like the annual rings in a section of a tree. It follows from this that the bands on the longer arcs (at the outside of the tree) are subject to greater stretching than those in the shorter arcs. I am talking of a section, which corresponds to a plank, because we most often encounter wood that way: in a log these bands would be concentric circles—and the strains would therefore be proportionately greater. This is why a log left to dry whole cracks so much more than one that is halved, or quartered.

The rule is then that the longer the annual rings in a plank, the more pull they have. The inherent tendency of wood sawn and then dried—by whatever method—is to warp towards the longer rings, the outside of the log. When you see a table-leaf that is wavy, or is warped in one sweep, remember this, and notice how the pieces were put together.

When you make a first cut in two- or three-inch-thick wood, watch carefully how the outside piece behaves. Usually it will spring, or begin to warp, during the cut or soon after. This first reaction will tell you whether the plank is driest inside (as when kiln-dried and then stored in damp air) or, as is more often the case, on the outside (air-dried wood).

Oak pieces sawn slash-grain at outside of log. Note spring, or bend, which is result of pent-up tensions in the tree itself. However dried, such wood is apt to misbehave.

Flitch-cut log of beechwood. The tendency to warp during the initial drying is towards the outside of the tree and its longer rings.

35

Part of what happens when you work with wood is foreseeable; a lot is not. That is why being stingy with wood can be disastrous. By playing it too close and re-sawing very nearly to the dimensions you finally will need, you may waste wood rather than saving it. If you allow only 1/16 inch on a six- or eight-inch-wide cut, and then the wood warps 1/8 inch, you will not be able to keep the dimensions you wanted. And 1/16 inch in a piece an inch or less thick makes a big difference: you can both see and feel it.

Therefore, allow for warpage. How much? Well, I should say that with what we can call "acceptably" dry wood—that is, wood you have bought and then aired and finally dried a while in your shop—you should allow almost 1/8 inch on a seven- or eight-inch-wide cut resulting in a piece 3/4 inch thick or less.

I am guessing. And you will be guessing. Which is why you should play it safe.

As you investigate your wood, remember it is seldom just what it appears to be! Color comes and goes, grain changes direction in different parts of a plank for mysterious reasons, knots play strange tricks, sometimes appearing almost out of nowhere, or, when you imagine they must go deep in the wood—they are in reality only on the surface, and quickly fade. There may be hidden pitch-pockets in the wood, and those ghastly honeycombs which improper kiln-drying can cause. Often cracks extend farther, and go deeper, than you've guessed.

Do I sound discouraging? I hope not. The truth is, I have had almost as many sorrows with wood as joys. And I'd like to spare you some of the sorrows

because I do not believe those who say that one has to make all the mistakes in the book in order to learn. For me, the more you care, the nicer the things you'd

Kiln-dried brown oak (three-inch plank here re-sawn) showing honeycombs.

like to make, the sadder it is to find—often too late—that you have simply misjudged your wood.

So be curious. Observe how the wood has been sawn; from what part of a log the plank or planks have come, whether or not the log was straight. Cut away the cracked end in order to better see how the annual rings go, and how the heart color— if there is one—seems to behave: whether it increases farther inside the plank or is present on one side or edge only.

This will be a first look; to feel more sure, you'll want to look again. "Worry" the wood. Give it no peace. Imagine the various parts of a plank, or planks, as parts of the thing you are going to make; and in your imagination play with all the possibilities. Try to fancy how the light or the dark in a plank would look in different parts of the piece you want to do; if there are frames to be made, panels, cabinet sides—think of the grain and colors, consider the shapes and proportions you'd like, and choose your wood accordingly.

With cabinet sides or parts of a panel, remember to allow a bit on the width at first, because as you look at the outside of the plank and the grain you are only guessing. When re-sawn, the insides may no longer quite correspond to your intention. By allowing extra on the width you are not wasteful; rather, you are giving yourself the chance to correct deviations by laying out the pieces a little bit askew— to one side or the other lengthwise—for your final cut.

Even with years of experience, one must concentrate when sawing the wood to size, since between hope and result there lies a line called attention.

You casually cross-cut a twelve-foot plank in two—it's apt to be six-foot halves. What are you going to do tomorrow, when you get a seven-foot idea?

Cross-cutting should always be preceded by careful thought.

It pays, when there is something of particular importance to be got out—such as frames for a pair of doors—frames that will determine the character of those doors and vitally affect a whole cabinet—to insure yourself against mishap by allowing for some extra pieces of wood. So, if you spoil one piece of a frame (easy to do when making joints!) that is going to balance its counterpart, you can replace it with an almost identical piece, one with the same balance of grain. Those doors are tremendously important for your idea. The success or failure of the cabinet depends upon keeping that idea alive. If you have no replacement and continue to make the cabinet you will become discouraged, and that will show in the piece. Afterwards, you might say, "It's a fair cabinet, but the doors could be better." This shows you are making demands on yourself, yes. But being aware of these demands earlier is more satisfying.

Of course, it does happen that unexpected things in the wood lead us to impulses and changes that result in a piece being even better than we hoped it would be: that is one of the rare adventures—and final satisfactions.

But it still pays to be cautious, not to play Russian roulette with your wood.

Caution is a presence for some of us who do this kind of work. My work has been called precise. Mere precision is often akin to engineering. Accurate machining, professional skill—with the attitude it requires. And that is not my way. If I'm precise—as I

can be—it is because I'm making something of which precision is a part. But only a part; there has to be something far more important. That I don't want to lose among accurate details. So I work neatly, almost gingerly at times, afraid to spoil a single detail of something I believe will be nice as a whole. In this case accuracy has not led to stiffness.

When you are on a track that is good and moving along, towards something you think will have delicacy, maybe grace, interesting proportions, and nice lines— if you're on to that you don't want to have to make any excuses, ever. No saying: The *lines* are fine, it looks all right from here, but next time I'll get the drawers to work more smoothly.

If I'm precise it is because I am trying to be consistent. To coax myself *all* the way, and no excuses. I am cautious almost to the point of paralysis. Afraid to spoil something, and get off the track. Oh, I am afraid: when I have the most wonderful wood, I flutter between delight and terror. Yet, I do go on, wanting that wholeness where nothing lets you down. Where your—and someone else's—impression will be without reservations.

People sometimes wonder at my patience. Truth is, I'm not a patient person. I'm an enthusiast. And when I get far enough into work I believe in, then time simply changes gears. It's that simple. It has to be—or you're walking a tightrope.

Patience? Think of oriental lacquer work. That is patience. As a way of life.

It is easy to say that we should know enough about wood to experience it as a whole, with all its properties of hardness or softness, of texture, color, and all the rest. We try to do so. And yet, I must admit that what tickles my woody fantasy most is color.

Color in wood is endlessly varied. Think of all the sorts of wood available to us and the scale of colors they represent; then imagine the range within each kind of wood from tree to tree—and finally consider some, only some, of the woods not quite accessible to us: then you begin to realize why wood is perhaps the richest of all craftsmen's materials. It's rich on the basis of color alone—even before we add its other physical properties.

Simply put, color is either directly related to the grain, which it follows—or it has a water-color effect, independent of the grain lines, shifting suggestively through the log and having only a general direction, or no direction at all. When it follows the grain, color is often darker in the heartwood, shifting to lighter in the sap, and in the shift are the most interesting parts of the wood. In some tropical woods there is a different relationship; with Andaman padouk, Indian laurel, and even doussie, for example, there is often an area of richer-colored wood quite far out towards the bark, while the heartwood can be a lighter, less pleasing shade.

Supposing you have discovered color that is very interesting and want to use it in a certain way: as the leaf of a table, the panels or sides for a cabinet, any important surface. Study that color pattern—one side and then the other of the plank—compare them, notice whether the grain tapers towards one end of the plank, and whether or not it slopes. Maybe the log was crooked, and there is a lessening of pattern in the middle area, with an increase towards the ends of the plank. Or just the opposite; only the middle part is exciting. Consider what might happen within the plank or planks: very often the patterns we finally obtain are not obvious on the surfaces, but there inside the wood. And we have several cuts to make.

So observe all these comings and goings, develop a guessing game with them. Keep in mind that *if the growth rings are flat or nearly flat with the surfaces, the color patterns usually change rapidly as you go beneath these surfaces.* Conversely, *if the rings are vertical, at or near right angles to the main surfaces and fairly parallel to these (no great rise or dip)—then any particular color going through the wood will be more predictable, its patterns and areas more alike on both sides of the plank.*

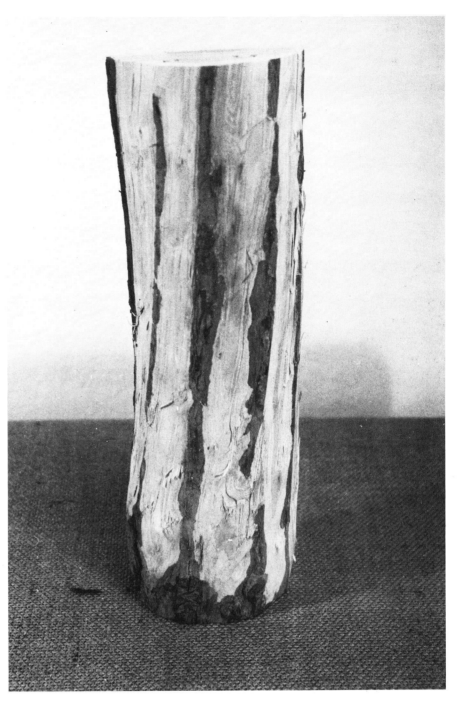

Applewood. Twist results in grain direction being different along the two outer edges of a flitch, with grain along the middle part fairly neutral.

39

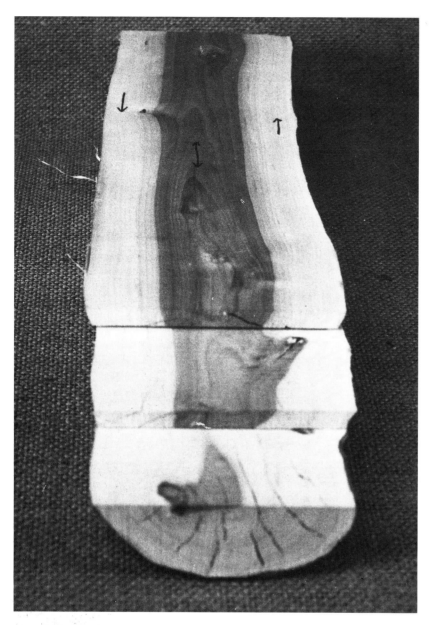

These photographs show how grain along the two opposite sides of a flitch can be different because of a twist in a log or tree. The grain at the middle, or heart (as shown above), is often neutral.

A miniature flitch-cut log (the apple-wood) showing changes in color, pattern, and their relationship when placed together in different ways.

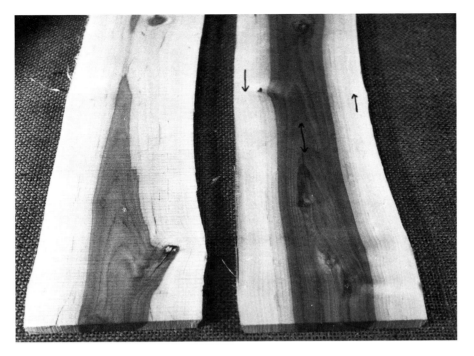

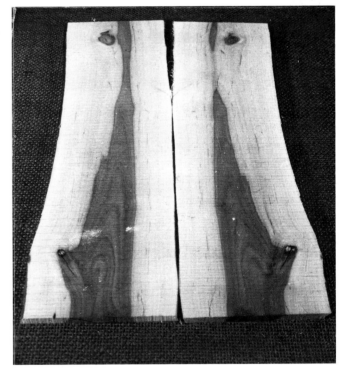

The watercolor effects in some woods, such as maple, old chestnut, or beech, will still be happily evasive. But even here you'll be able to make some use of this rule, or, more accurately, this fundamental observation, which will be important in many situations, some of which I will discuss later.

Sometimes we come upon planks with just a touch of color left on one rough-sawn surface—often, as I mentioned, this was a cut near the last of the heartwood. In the United States and Canada, where wood is mostly random sawn and stored, any plank in a pile may be touched with color, especially since much of this wood is slash-grained.

If the plank is warped we have a special problem. We notice a lovely pattern, we see by the end-grain that it goes a tiny bit into the wood and then disappears. And we like this pattern: a greenish splash on maple, a speck of crimson in pearwood, a wisp of brownish smoke in a piece of applewood. A flicker of discoloration: elusive, fanciful. The question is how to save it? What to do with this crooked piece of wood? If you try to machine the patterned surface flat, you lose the color—a quarter of an inch, perhaps only an eighth of an inch and it is gone.

Don't machine that surface! Hand-plane it, following the warp; if possible, make careful saw-cuts on each side of the color (so as not to spoil its pattern) right through the plank. Then re-saw to a thickness which is suitable for, let us say, a single door containing that rare pattern. An odd, fascinating door, a bit twisted yes—but so nice! The beginning of an unexpected cabinet. The germ of a finished piece in that little bit of color which might so easily have been lost: having saved it you are involved in work which will form itself spontaneously around that idea. You may or may not use the colorless rest of the plank, that's unimportant now. You have been touched by the spark of color in a piece of wood which an hour earlier did not exist. Work in its warmth. Be wasteful if need be: in such a case it's an enjoyable waste.

If it feels right, allow yourself to be sidetracked by a single wisp of color in a plank. This won't be according to the habits of efficiency and the trade and competition—but it may be the final justification for our kind of craftsman to keep going uphill.

Yes, preserve that precious little pattern. Get from it the inspiration which will help you to make a piece someone will enjoy—someone who will share your discovery and your joy through that piece.

Of all the light-colored woods, maple is my favorite. (There is a commercial variety of this wood in Europe which is rather uninteresting: aside from this, most maple is worth looking into.) It is more exciting than its reputation. Maple makes its own, special demands on any cabinetmaker with an eye for subtleties. Here the color changes can be as tricky as they are fascinating: sometimes soft and watery, shifting slowly from sap to darker heart as if through a fog. Again, there can be a rich greenish streak separating the two, and then swirls of dark green and mauve at the center of the trees. So much happens with this wood! Including the unpredictable and frustrating cracks, shakes—often hardly discernible—in or near the heart area. You think you have a great piece of maple—fantastic patterns—maybe you even begin to work it, before you discover those faults. They are microscopic, they come and go, disappear—only to be there again. Diabolically small, they may fool your eye, but seldom your fingertips. So beware! Look and *feel* your way.

Maple is seldom if ever quite the same tone in two logs. Watch out: looking at the mill-sawn rough surface is usually deceiving. Cut a bit under it to find the true shade; the oxidized rough after-saw surface can be a sixteenth of an inch or so deep. Don't just scrape the wood—cut into it a bit. Another point: maple is one of the woods where a prismatic effect is most noticeable. *This effect is to all purposes not directly the result of grain, but rather the way the fibers themselves respond to, or refract, the light.* If you are going to book-match pieces of maple—especially those from the sapwood—then take into account this typical light-and-dark effect. Since most trees twist as they grow, not only the grain but also the refractions are seldom the same along both outside edges of a wide "whole" plank. This effect is less noticeable in some planks (or logs) than in others,

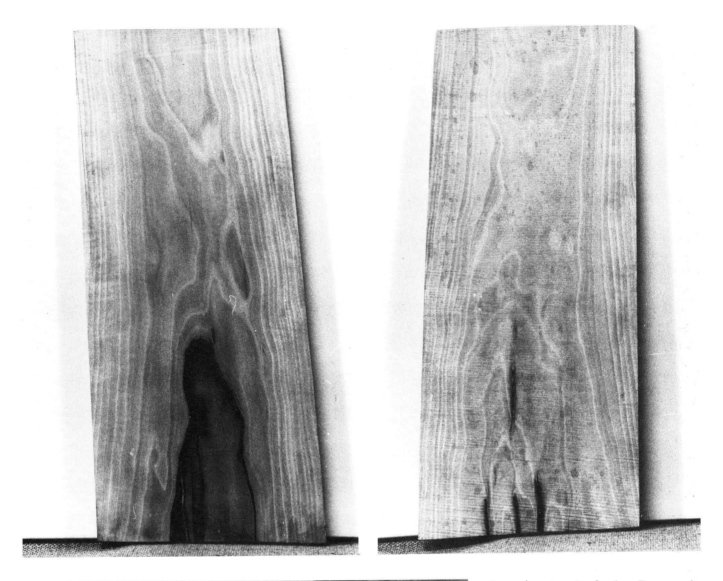

A precious touch of color. Pearwood.

and hardly a bother in the darker heartwood, but it nearly always is there to be reckoned with.

Obviously, if you want the shifting impression of book-matching this (or any such) wood, it is not a problem: we know that a re-sawn and book-matched plank of maple gives a light-dark combination. Also there is no use trying to up-end one of the halves—the contrast will still be there because the direction of fibers has not changed! But if you now spin the one half around, and place its other edge to the first half as it is, you get a calmer surface— calm, that is, if the pattern of the grain and the shade allows such a turn-around matching. Which it may not do, since the color of maple usually becomes successively lighter towards the outside of the tree.

See how much trouble this wood can cause?

A hint along with the warning: if you want a calm effect, try to match heart-to-heart whenever you can.

We are back now to an earlier observation about color and pattern in relation to various cuts:

If *the growth rings slope or are in arcs to the surfaces the patterns will match only when the two newly opened halves are placed edge to edge. These patterns will "leave" one another as we plane or mill the surface.*

Two sides of half-plank (or random-sawn plank). The heartwood decreases toward the outside of the log. The pattern of the re-sawn halves will be "in-between" these two.

Does this really matter? Well, let's put it this way: if you *intend* two halves of a definite pattern to match, and they *almost but not quite* do match—it probably does matter, yes. Because nothing catches the eye as does that "not quite." But if you simply throw the pieces together—then what does matter at all? Continuing now: on the two back sides, the patterns can be disturbingly different: a book-matched door or panel may look fine closed—and ugly when opened.

With vertical-sawn wood, the patterns on the re-sawn and then matched halves "follow" one another as we work the surfaces, and even the back sides of these are quite similar.

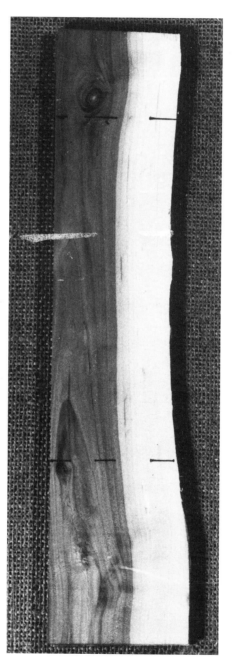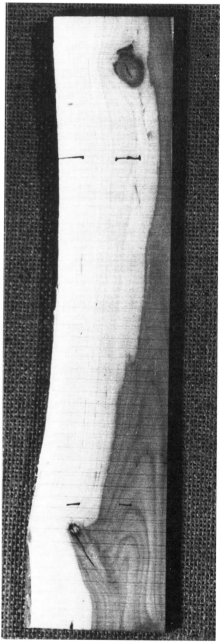

44

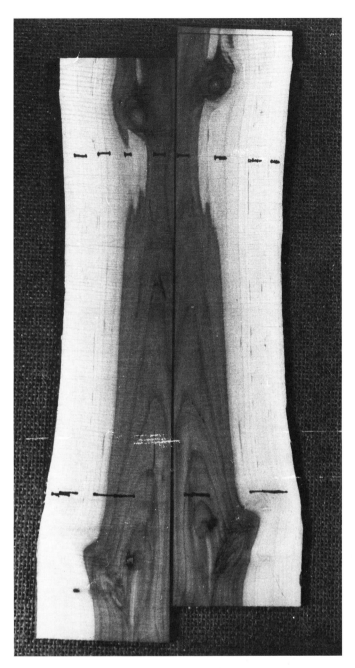

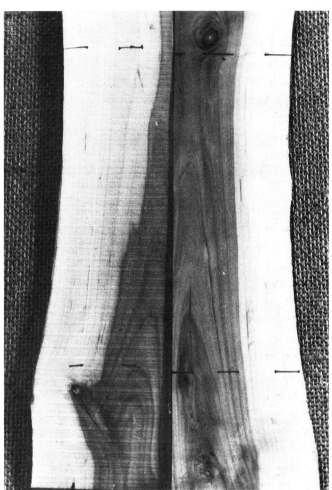

Half-plank opened (re-sawn). Even with a bandsaw, the cut results in a loss of pattern—the two halves must be shifted a bit to regain balance.

Back of the same re-sawn plank. The differences in pattern are apparent and often disturbing.

As to direction of grain, keep in mind: *when book-matched, all definite direction of grain has its opposite in the other half of a re-sawn piece.* This can cause problems in the middle area, along the joint. Work the two half surfaces as close to a finish as possible before gluing them together, and keep them flush when you glue.

Book-matching is a way of obtaining larger surfaces and patterns out of random-sawn and relatively (though not always) narrow planks. It is something which you sooner or later should get used to doing.

Personally, I find the results a bit monotonous. An alternative to book-matching is to work *across* a plank (flitch) wide enough to give you the entire surface you want. This can be very stimulating: you play with balance and rhythm rather than the often all-too-perfect symmetry of book-matching. There is more life and, to me, more meaning in a fine flitch-cut surface. Provided, of course, that it is the right kind of plank—wide enough, cut at a part of the log where the wood is interesting. Which is asking for a lot from an ordinary supplier! (Here again a portable mill may be the solution.)

To get back to maple. It has knots; more than some of the big-tree tropical woods available to us. Small knots can be an asset, or a bother, depending. Asset or bother, they are often a puzzle. We know that they generally fan out from the heart (wherever *that* is in odd-sawn wood!) at about right angles to the rings. In a flat-grained piece they should, if they obey the rules, go straight through: in a vertical-grain piece, knots are supposed to be fairly with the flat. But are they? How far does this knot continue? Does it turn as it goes? Is it cracked, is the wood around it cracked? Your guess is as good as mine. Probably better. Be careful; the better the wood, the more careful. One way to go about this is to proceed by stages. You have looked at the wood time and again. Re-

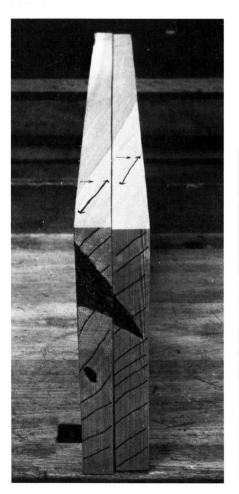

Pearwood book-match. Note how grain, unless flat, assumes different directions in two halves of the resulting surface.

A (miniature) wide flitch—"across-the-log" cut. One can select a desired pattern and work without having to book-match, provided the width is sufficient.

46

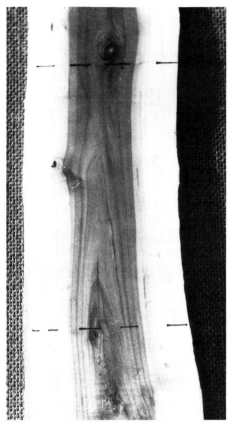

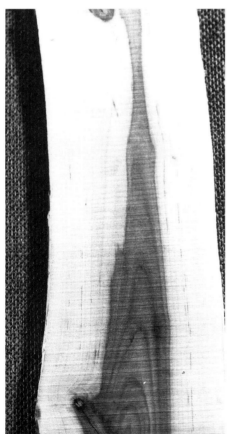

gardless of whether you have a definite piece to make, or a first idea, you sense what you are looking for, have a fair image of the colors and shapes, the *mood* you want.

Develop the habit of caution. Divide the most important elements of the piece, and the wood for these, into a relationship that makes sense. Making a cabinet with unbroken surfaces, you'll be more interested in wood with color than in wood which is plain. You may envisage the way it should be, the door or doors with ripples of color to enhance surface and shape, the sides in some interesting relation to the front.

Concentrate on these. Re-saw first the wood for those doors. Look for faults; look again. Then saw what you need for the sides. Study what you have. Now, maybe, make those doors—just to be sure this most important part is right. Take another step: a back piece with frame and panel may be more vital than the top and bottom pieces; choose the wood for the panel with this in mind. If you are sure all is as you want it, go on sawing for the other parts: top, bottom, shelves, etc. If you are lucky and have more than enough wood, lay some aside—just in case. Or even saw an extra piece of some critical part. This may sound like waste, but, I repeat, it really is not; it's a way to work more calmly towards better results.

Getting into this matter of listening to wood, of composing, weaving together an intention with what you and your chosen wood have to say, is an experience difficult to describe. To me, it is the essence of working with wood.

A painter or sculptor visits a certain place and sees and feels something there he wants to interpret: a person, a scene, the way the light falls. A time and a place. A sense of life. Something similar happens with the cabinetmaker—he who is more than a maker of cabinets. He has an idea, maybe a sketch. A boxlike object with a few gentle curves whose meaning he only guesses. Or a more sculptural piece where he imagines the play of light on shapes; serious or with humor, difficult or easy. And there before him is the wood he has chosen. Wood—and with it a mood.

Then within this mood, all these other aspects: the shadings, accents, tensions—that which corresponds to the painter's inspiration and later on, often much later, all those bevels, roundings, shapes within shapes which will clarify and enhance what has been an intention and a hope.

This sounds involved. With a subtle wood like maple it *is* involved: working thus, you are committing yourself to getting the very best out of a material that should mean a great deal to you. With care, concentration, and luck you will do justice to that material.

A potter has remarked that there are the forces of the universe in a revolving bit of clay. True. Likewise real for some of us is the mystery of the pattern of a flower or a blade of grass in an open piece of old maple.

I mentioned that one should keep wood in the conditions of the workshop for as long as possible before using it. This applies no matter where the wood originally came from: whether you have taken it from the log and kept it in various stages of drying for several years—or have brought in some supposedly dry wood from a lumberyard, and stored it indoors for a few months. Between storage in your shop and final usage you must allow for still one more stage—relatively short but often frustrating—namely, the "settling down" that follows re-sawing.

If you are going to work with solid wood, and do it without undue trouble, you simply must form the habit of planning so as to allow two or three weeks (generally) for this final acclimatization of the wood before starting work on the piece itself.

Very likely you will be re-sawing at least some of your wood. Have a place in the shop where you can stack the re-sawn pieces. A wooden rack that you can move around or later take down is good for this. Keep the wood up off the floor, in normally dry air. Stack it properly, use thin sticks (1/8 or 3/16 inch) to save space, and then keep an eye on it for that week or two or three—in time you will know which. Don't push it! Work on something else, and wait for this wood; make it a habit to do so.

Re-sawn stock "settling" on rack in workshop.

Watch for warpage in the pieces you've sawn. Earlier I explained the natural tendency of wood is to warp towards the outside of a log and the longer growth rings. To this generalization I should now add another: *the so-called natural warpage is reliable only when the wood is fairly even in its dryness or moisture*, as when it is first milled or after it has been completely dried. Almost all the wood we have in our shop is somewhere in between: it is almost, but not quite, dry. If the plank is two or three inches thick, there will definitely be a difference in humidity between the outside and the inside wood. This nearly dry wood with its slightly uneven moisture content will warp when re-sawn. More or less, but it will warp. And the warpage will not be only in the direction of the outside or longer growth rings— though it may be. *The main cause of warpage now is uneven moisture: the pieces will, after being re-sawn, tend mainly to warp towards the surface that is less dry.* In the case of air-dried wood this is usually towards the inside of a thick piece that has been opened. With kiln-dried wood that is stored afterwards in fairly humid air, the process has begun to reverse: the first cut may tend to warp or even spring outward.

If some of the re-sawn pieces

48

are warping badly, remove these from the stack and place them two-by-two together with the concaves of warpage face to face. In pairs like this they will let less air on the surfaces that are turned inward, and more on the others, and perhaps they'll straighten out some—although it is too much to hope that they will be completely straight or flat. The purpose here is to slow down further warpage.

Normally, after two or three weeks the wood should be calm enough for you to be able to proceed with your work. Note: I say "normally." Which means the wood is for your purposes dry when you re-saw it.

"This chap is asking us to fuss with wood!" someone will say. "He is slowing everything beyond reason."

Yes, I am asking you to fuss with wood. To form what some regard as fussy habits. As to going beyond reason—that is something each of you will determine when the time is right.

Two halves of re-sawn Indian laurel-wood warped toward new cut because they were more moist inside—rather than warping with the annual rings only, as would be the case with wood with the same moisture throughout.

Newly re-sawn wood should be stacked with even access of air. Left on bench it will warp. When turned over in attempt to correct such warp—it may return only part way, since it is already drier than when first resawn.

Like people, various sorts of wood have their nationalities, their tribes and families. And, like people, wood has personality. No two trees, nor even two pieces of wood, are quite alike—not if you know them well enough. Scientific names, classifications, and descriptions I am vague about, though I have experienced some properties of wood at first hand. And like anyone interested enough in his work I have found at least some of the good and the bad that is worth sharing.

For most of us who work with it, there is friendly wood and unfriendly wood. Granted, that depends on what kind of work you do. If you are a woodcarver, or a turner, then cherry is wonderful. It is one of the classic woods for carving—at least in the Far East. Pearwood is really special; it has a firm, even texture, very little or almost no true grain, so that the wood is easily worked in any direction (*if* the tools are truly sharp). There are lovely shadings in natural unbleached pearwood: it is ivory or mauve or sometimes pinkish in color, very mild. (The more common, commercial, steamed pearwood has a reddish tone; there is less life in it. It is fairly homogeneous in color—and thus better suited to production work. The unsteamed pear has more charm—but is less predictable.) Both natural and steamed pearwood are fine for cutting and shaping, and make excellent chairs for someone who

is sensitive enough to coax the best shadings out of the wood and work with delicate shapes. But because pearwood has almost no distinct fibers it lacks strength cross-grain, so that if you use it with mortise-and-tenon joints they will not be strong. To make proper joints for a pearwood chair (or similar piece) you should use doweling throughout, or, if you want to make tenons these ought to be another kind of wood—stronger than pear. Such tenons are inserted into slots made in both parts of the joint with the help of a horizontal mortising machine. This sounds technical, but is not difficult to do. What *is* difficult is to conceive and then make a chair that is delicate in its appeal—and yet strong, as a chair should be.

Wood means various things to various craftsmen. A maker of musical instruments, for instance, has an entirely different

approach to wood than does a maker of chairs, or of cabinets. His attitude is similar in that he is very sensitive to the mysteries of wood, but his use of wood, the meaning of wood to his work, is quite different. For him (as for a boatbuilder who makes fine wooden masts), spruce may be the most important of all woods. Spruce to many of us is very common, uninteresting, matter-of-fact wood. The maker of violins or guitars knows intimately other properties of spruce. He is aware that the finest spruce for the sounding boards of such instruments grows on the continent of Europe, somewhere in Bavaria or Austria, on the slopes of certain mountains, at a certain altitude, where the wind blows from a certain direction and the soil has specific characteristics. And the process of obtaining this wood, seasoning it, caring for it, and finally selecting the few pieces that will be

Mortise for hardwood tenon where wood in rest of piece has little cross-grain strength (fractures easily).

used is something of a ritual. It is more than a science: it is closer to religion. It is beautiful, the way these really fine instrument makers live with their wood. Besides spruce, rosewood, curly maple, and even other sorts of maple are also very important to them. These they will select with almost the same care as the spruce. Woven together with the sensitivity of the instrument maker are what I would like to call the feelings of the wood. And the result, with the help of incantations and various secret processes, is a fine musical instrument.

Now how do you appreciate such an instrument except through wonderful music?

A craftsman making supple, bent-wood forms, perhaps chairs and even laminated sculpture, is interested in quite different properties of wood. Maybe his favorite wood is ash, or hickory, or fine-grained oak: these are ideal for bending. So is beechwood. But again there are exceptions: if it is a matter of strain and hard wear, as in a chair, then of course ash, hickory, oak, or beech should be used. If it is to be a bent-wood sculpture that is merely viewed, put on exhibition or kept somewhere protected in one's home, then the strength of the wood is not all that important, provided it can be cut into thin enough laminations to make the forms one wants.

To our carver, any wood that has a rowed structure—with the grain sloping in strips alternately one way and another—is a bother and an irritation: it is what he and I would call unfriendly wood. We will not be happy trying to do good carving in such wood—though it can be done. Here we like pearwood, which the craftsman doing lamination probably thinks is inferior.

Among woods that are typically rowed are padouk, afromosia, doussie, bubinga, wenge, and cocobolo. These are tropical woods, which is not to say that all rowed wood comes from the tropics.

For most of us cabinetmakers working mainly with surfaces and proportions, a general direction of the grain is very helpful. In rowed wood it is partly against us whichever surface or shape we are trying to bring forth; especially if we are working with handtools such as planes, knives, and chisels. As a result, if we are going to make furniture out of these rowed woods, our feelings and our idea must be such from the start that we are prepared to use our machines as much as possible—then do our surfaces and shapes with cutting tools as far as we can—after which we should be willing to labor with a cabinetscraper and perhaps files, and finally do some sanding. We must accept the facts

Typical rowed wood (Andaman padouk). Grain in alternating strips is raised when planing. Such wood is best worked with scraper (below) and then sanded to finish.

of our wood, and adjust to them. If from the beginning we are set upon carving and planing, then early in the work we will be frustrated by rowed wood—even though it *does* look nice. This will reflect on us and on the results.

Knowing what to expect from a given kind of wood is important: we weigh this against what we want to do with it. Sometimes this means making compromises. A gorgeous piece of Andaman padouk does not easily lend itself to our planes— we know that now. But maybe we have something in mind with a lot of curves, bevels, fancy shapes which we imagine would look fine in this padouk. *Now* it is easier for us to become eager about the work and the wood. We can postpone the calm therapy of planing—forget a certain cabinet or table for a while—and get at the task of handling that padouk, working in quite a different way.

Somewhere we have to decide. Tune in on the part of us which must work, and work well. The incentive might be an exciting idea involving forms: we are willing to wrestle a hard, rowed red wood to see it through.

Another time we feel different: we've been close to a plank of exquisite cherry, discovered a pattern that would suit—yes, *make*—a great table-leaf which we could plane to a shimmering, live surface. Now we don't want to compromise. So we forget wild shapes, and do that table, and are happy doing it.

At the same time as we consider any wood from the point of working with it, we try to associate with the use of the object we plan to make: its function, the construction this involves, and how the piece will behave. Some of us like to imagine ourselves as the users of our pieces— even if we can't afford to own them. We also find it natural to be aware of time and what it will do to the wood and to the piece as a whole.

A few woodworkers shrug. "Well, whatever happens to the wood will be a natural process." This is true, though an oversimplification. I think that those of us who can't help worrying about the future of the objects we make, and want them to age gracefully, want also to know enough about the wood we use to be able to predict some of what will happen later on.

Most wood darkens with time. How quickly and how much depends upon the kind of wood, the finish (if any) and the amount of exposure to sunlight. There are exceptions however—Indian rosewood, for instance, loses its rich tones and turns grayish in daylight, and a number of the non-tropical woods such as ash and elm darken very little.

Wood darkens with varying degrees of grace. Padouk from the Andaman Islands and India turns from red or orange to a rich, deep reddish brown. The more common African padouk is at first a brilliant tomato red, really a knockout color, which those of us who know recognize as false: this African padouk will, within half a year, become the color of muddy water! Un-

less you realize that such a change will occur, and include it in the future of the piece you make, then you and someone else are in for a deep disappointment.

This brings me to the matter of finishes and when to use them, or when not to use them. Ash and elm will not change much through the years, provided you don't smear something on them. They are nice woods, and it is a shame to see them treated with oil or lacquer which turns them an unpleasant, "wet" yellow. Left natural, elm and ash are beautiful; they look fine hand-planed, or planed and then sanded very lightly so as to give a misty effect. *Any* finish put on such wood will detract from rather than add to it.

Maple darkens somewhat when oiled, less if it is waxed. If you wish to accentuate the usual yellowish color or a pattern of greenish heartwood, you should use oil—with or without oil-based wax. Again: if the wood pattern is delicate and the piece holds some of that delicacy (as it should), you can help it along by using a synthetic English wax called Renaissance, which enhances the mildness in wood, protects it, and gives a sensitive finish. Use this wax sparingly!

Cherrywood is difficult for me to comment upon. The American variety is definitely reddish, and I find it not always clear in color. It darkens quickly and assumes a tone that is foreign to my taste. I am used to the European cherry with its greenish yellow tones, mild and often clear. It takes oil or wax very well, without darkening too much, and in time becomes a warm honey color. Admittedly this is a bias on my part: the American cherry has its own appeal.

In walnut I find a parallel to cherry, in that there is such a difference between the European—the classic Italian and French walnut—and the North American. European walnut at its best (such wood is extremely hard to find now) is milder in texture and tone, with more variety of subdued colors; pinkish, gray, and mauve, than is its American relative. The latter is definitely darker and often of a purplish shade; it takes oil fairly well—if you want walnut that looks heavier and more sober. The European sort is mild even when oiled—though I like it best untreated, or perhaps waxed a little.

Wood can change color very drastically when oiled. In fact, it sometimes assumes a quite different character. Natural pearwood often has a wavy shift; when worked by hand with fine cutting tools it is very subtle in its shimmer and luster. If you treat it with oil, a complete change takes place: the color becomes a much darker tan, the shimmer is gone, and there is a splotchy effect which may appeal to some tastes, but is definitely no longer delicate. Steamed pearwood, a fairly even reddish color at first, will also become darker and somewhat uneven when oiled or treated with an oil-based wax. Neither gives what I would call a refined effect, though in turned pieces (bowls, etc.) this finish is often interesting. If you are mak-

ing something to be placed alongside antique furniture, then maybe steamed pearwood with an oil-and-wax finish, nicely polished, will solve somebody's problem.

Doussie and mahogany appreciate an oil finish. Doussie wood is not much used in furniture nowadays. A pity, because it is a fine stable wood that dries easily, has beautiful end grain and a coarse-haired structure. Strange thing, supply and demand: I met a wood dealer in London who had spent six years in West Africa. "Ah, yes, everything was doussie there. Panels, furniture, floors, everything. Great wood, doussie." Yes, it is. It shows a yellowish-pink shade when first opened, and then turns towards red and brown, there being a difference between various logs. Now and then I have come upon planks with a ripple of red and orange, though most of what is available is an even beige color which in time turns dark brown. Doussie has a masculine air about it: you can imagine it in a library or conference room somewhere. Aged, it is a very elegant wood, and if you compare it with mahogany— the kinds of mahogany available today, that is—you will notice the elegance of the one and the rather commonplace appearance of the other.

Cuban mahogany is long since gone, and the mahogany we get now is uninteresting. It does not have the firm texture or give the fine surface we associate with real mahogany. Still—it is a "good" wood, if you can find the best mahogany available; the

Philippine and Honduras works easily enough when it isn't rowed. African mahogany usually is rowed, has an anemic look and a mealy texture. If you still want to use it, remember: rowed wood appears even more striped when oiled or waxed.

You will have guessed that mahogany is not among my favorite woods, though it might have been. Once long ago I did have some real Cuban mahogany; only a few pieces, the last of what an old boatbuilder had gotten years earlier. Compared to that, any other mahogany is a disappointment.

A wood like Rio rosewood— if and when you can get it, that is—will suffer from an oily finish. No, this wonderful deep brown and blackish wood should not be oiled. It can perhaps be synthetic-waxed. There is still another finish, which I have not yet mentioned, that would go well with this wood. If you want almost no change in tone, and wish still to seal the pores somewhat and protect the wood from finger smudges and dust, then you can use a fine old traditional finish—namely, polish: the original furniture polish one might call it. This consists of shellac and alcohol, and is simple to use.

We used to be able to get shellac in dry form, bleached and unbleached flakes or powder, the bleached being almost colorless, while the unbleached was the common orange shellac. In school we got our shellac, some pure alcohol, empty bottles reminiscent of strong beverages, and a funnel—and then went through

53

a sort of ritual, a classic process learned in the trade, of diluting the shellac in alcohol. You let the mixture stand for a few weeks, shaking it now and then—and poured off the clear liquid through a gauze filter, after which you added more alcohol. How much? Ah, now, that we all guessed while pretending to know. We had our concoction in a bottle—or bottles (this was more impressive)—for a long time, there being a saying that like certain liquors, polish gained through age. True or untrue, what does it matter when you have experienced the aura? We would shake our bottles, hold them against the light, and gaze sagely to judge whether or not the magic liquid was ready to use.

There is a simpler way of making polish. Buy a can of ready-mixed commercial shellac, either the white or the orange. Pour part of it—say about a third—into another container, and then add to this about two parts by volume of alcohol. After a day or so this mixture will separate into a clear saturated solution and some residue. Carefully pour off the clear liquid—and add to this about one part by volume of alcohol. To those who have not used polish, this may seem alarmingly thin. Don't worry; it *should* be thin—it is not intended to be a thick coating on the wood. Applying it is almost like putting on coats of pure alcohol. Polish dries very quickly, and if you use bleached shellac it leaves the wood almost unchanged in color. Orange shellac is best for wood

with a tendency towards red. Experiment with mixtures and observe the results.

Use a soft cloth to apply the polish, work evenly with light sweeps from the middle area and towards the ends of a surface, *with* the grain always. Sand very lightly between coats, and wipe away the dust each time. After four or five treatments you build up a thin, almost imperceptible coating and a nice luster. Don't choke the wood with a heavier solution.

A well-polished surface is lustrous but not glossy. It responds to the hand—one really feels the wood there—and keeps its luster while protecting the surface against dust. But remember: polish is very susceptible to moisture, so it is not ideal for ordinary table-tops and other furniture that might be exposed to liquids.

An advantage of polish is that it is sweet-smelling year after year. Some oils and waxes used on the inside of cabinets or drawers become rancid in time and emit an unpleasant odor. Yet many people do not mind the odor of old oil or of some of the lacquer finishes—which shows how used we are to such smells. But it is nice to approach a well-made piece of furniture, open a door or drawer, see the mild color of the wood inside—and smell the aroma of polish. I think that almost anyone, regardless of experience, will be pleasantly surprised by the fragrance and the texture.

The natural aroma of certain woods is also important to me. If I am making drawers and

have some Lebanon cedar, or juniper, or Asian padouk, I certainly do not want to seal the wood inside and, with any finish, seal in that fascinating smell. I hope the smell of a very special wood will be a part of experiencing the piece later on.

When I speak of treating wood with oil I am thinking of hardwoods, and the oil I have in mind is one of the fine Danish furniture oils—Dyrups teak oil. It is similar to an American oil called Watco. Though I believe the Danish brand is superior, this is of course subject to discussion. At any rate, I'm referring to this oil in connection with hardwoods, mostly the tropical ones.

If you are working with oak or fir or some of the other coarse-grained, softer woods, you can very well use linseed oil or various mixtures of oil and wax. The number of patent formulas and deep dark secrets is almost as great as the number of truly interested cabinetmakers. There is no universal solution, no do-it-all. One can safely assume that some woods benefit by oil, others lose by it. Oil brings out the yellow in light-colored wood, and deepens the shades of red and brown in others. Whatever finish you use, have a piece of the wood in question on hand as a sample. Treat this, put it in sunlight for a while, watch it, treat it again—and think!

I do not discuss other finishes simply because I know too little about them. I don't use them. The thought of lacquer and all sorts of synthetic solutions that seal the wood, that preserve it for eternity, or prevent it from drying, or assure absolute and complete protection against anything and everything—this is enough to keep me from these finishes and the attitudes they represent.

For whatever reasons—smell, color, feel—wood as it is after being worked with skill is for me a matter of pride, almost a boast. Many of the pieces I make are intentionally of wood that need not be sanded—or even finished at all.

Cabinetmakers who make mostly cabinets are apt to be interested in surfaces rather than in shapes, in proportions and volume rather than in curves. For us the fineness of lines—a shading or a thin profile—is of great importance. We do what might be called a subdued sort of sculpture: framed among those lines and gentle surfaces we like to have wood with suggestive patterns.

I am forever looking for pieces with unusual patterns and colors: pieces that have been subjected to moisture and are stained, or are still sound though on the verge of decay. Here is a tiny dark cloud of heartwood left; there the heart and sapwood meet to form an interesting swirl. A knot has produced a tense curve in the grain: I will use that tensed grain though not necessarily the knot itself, which is loose. Nor other faults such as cracks, and blue fungus, and rot in the wood.

When do we cease listening to wood, and begin to exploit it? Hard to say. It is difficult to take a stand on this—other than in relation to your own judgment and your attitude towards your craft.

Some woodworkers do use naturally striking defects as effects, and a few of them do this rather well. I know that in larger pieces, and especially sculptured ones, this can be justified. More often it is a form of opportunism, of doing less subtle work and then letting the originality of the wood compensate for the fact that one has not worked better. What is better? Well, again I am at a loss, except to ask: doesn't that, too, depend on each of us?

Besides wood with what we can call surface appeal, there is wood that we remember because it wears beautifully. Elm, for instance—handled in the right way it will become more and more pleasing as the years go by. If you have seen a real antique Windsor chair, or any very old chair made out of elm, you will understand what I mean: at the seat and along the armrests, where the original finish is gone, there is the wood itself with its coarse grayish brown color and natural sheen. To me, no other part of a chair, however bright, is half as fine as those worn parts with the patina which decades of cloth-against-wood has brought forth.

Don't choose elm for a coffee table unless you want to lacquer it—which I hope you do not. But elm is a most suitable wood for a chair, and if I made a chair of elm, I would not protect the wood at all, but would expect the owner to appreciate the fact that

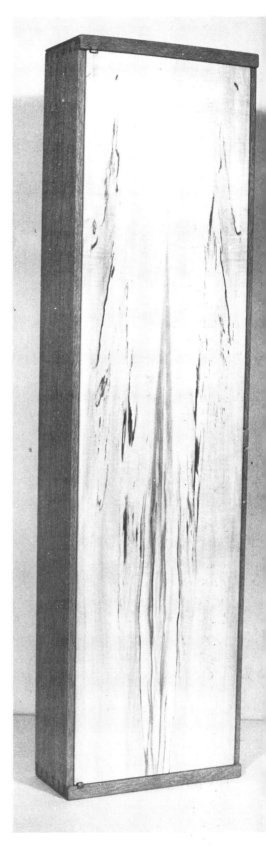

Wall cabinet in Swedish chestnut (door) and oak. Height about thirty inches.

55

as the chair became worn it would acquire a patina and thus be enriched as the years passed.

Scientific knowledge about wood is available to us. Latin names, photos of leaves and bark, tables of moisture content, diagrams of ways wood is cut (do we have a choice?), the time per inch of thickness it takes for certain woods to dry, the predicted shrinkage and warping of woods—these we are given. Yet much of this knowledge is so precise as to be impersonal, distant—it does not always apply to us and the conditions under which we live and work. Because even while it is true that wood should be stored in certain ways and used when at a given percentage of humidity, it is also true that any of these facts have to be applied and interpreted by the individual.

To see, according to a table of figures, that one kind of wood will shrink twice as much as another is certainly beneficial. But what then? How will these woods "live" in a finished piece during the four seasons?

Some of us will become involved in tables and instruments, percentages of this and that. The tendency to engineer our relationship with wood begins in education. On the other hand there is know-how, the old, commonsense experiences upon which rest most of the rules governing the good, sound, long-lasting pieces of cabinetmaking—old as well as new, fact tempered by humility.

Somewhere I read something to the effect that having dried wood to the proper moisture content and then built something out of it, some consideration should be given to future moisture exchange with the atmosphere. That was the order: you make a thing, and *then* consider how the wood will come and go! Moreover, I read, if your design hasn't been good (it won't be, with that order of things!), then you should seal the finished piece so as to prevent exchange of moisture.

Well, if this is how you think, you should build with plastics. Because trying to prevent the natural breathing of a cabinet with several doors and drawers is like trying to keep a person from breathing—you have to kill him or her in order to succeed.

This is one of the reasons why we have so much arty furniture that is nice but, alas, falling apart. And other work that is still together—under all kinds of chemical gloss and color.

Seriously, let us know our wood as we do our hands, and work with it in common respect and harmony. I can't tell you how—that goes way back, and is there for us even when we are up-to-date, design conscious and even original. But I do believe this: good design in our work must contain commonsense, and humility—besides what we call knowledge.

Let me state clearly that I do not exclude, or deride, being scientific about these matters. Knowing the specific weight of various woods, weighing them and keeping track of them as they dry, using a moisture-meter—all this is legitimate. In a production unit, the meter can be a necessity. Only keep in mind: for the lone craftsman such an approach can become an involvement that is binding, time-consuming—and finally, confusing. A carver may have two dozen wood flitches, easily accessible, and he can keep "exact" track of these. Another person has stacks and piles of wood all over the place; for him the same exact method might lead to chaos.

Exact measurement is not always meaningful. Here are two pieces of ash from the same supplier, bought together. One is half again as heavy as the other. More moist? Or a difference in the hardness of the wood? A difference which will always be there and that one needs to sense, and live with, and use properly.

A man in a boat off-soundings has the sun, the stars, a changing moon, the shifting shades of sea-moods. And he reads these life-signs. The master on the bridge of a supertanker has his signs too: blinking panel-lights and trembling dials and a voice from two thousand miles away. Who can say which is the sailor, the seaman, or simply a man at sea? Personally, I'd prefer to be that chap in his own boat.

Your workshop may be very dry, drier than the places where the various pieces you make will live. You make them in that cozy dry shop; then the pieces go to people whose homes are more humid—and unpleasant things happen. The wood begins to swell; it buckles; something pops. You are unhappy. So are the owners of the pieces.

The opposite extreme brings other griefs: your shop may be in a really humid basement or a barn. You do your work in that nice cool place—and then it goes to homes that are steam-heated, very dry indeed. The wood dries and warps, joints let go.

It is dishonest and inexcusable to overlook these matters and say: "Well, I make the pieces the best way I can. If they are subjected to different conditions later on, that's not my fault." Or, as one artist-craftsman told someone who complained over a cracked chair, "I make the stuff, I don't repair it."

It seems more proper, and it certainly is more satisfying, to be aware and develop a sense of balance in your work: feel how dry the wood is, keep the shop moderately dry and well ventilated, know how the things one makes will act later on. It is gratifying to observe all this as time passes, and learn, and make objects that are not a disappointment to anyone, objects that do not misbehave.

Thus, our craft can bring us in tune with the seasons. The time of the year you make a piece determines the tolerances you allow in the various working parts—yes, actually *how* you make them. In some climates there is a great deal of difference between winter and summer humidity: very likely you use certain constructions which the experience of craftsmen before you has shown to be right for such conditions. (Though I suspect that a misuse of this know-how is leading to some of the oversimplified and downright clumsy pieces we see around us.)

In other climates the humidity is more constant: there you do not need to worry so much about what time of the year it is when you work.

For our purposes, let's say that different seasons do bring different degrees of moisture, and that allowing for these differences belongs to the pride and honest enjoyment of cabinetmaking. Part of this tuning in is a matter of patience. It is the way you approach your work, people, life. If you make things hastily, you are less apt to consider the future of the things you make. If you do coarse, heavy-handed work, then tolerances are less important to you than for someone who does delicate pieces that have a highly strung temperament of their own.

It takes a long time to do the latter sort of work, but if you do it, then a part of your feeling must be the wish for these pieces to live a good life. You don't want to make excuses for them.

This I think comes gradually to one; it comes through mistakes and sensitivity and the ability to accumulate experiences. But it does not come at all if you have no pride.

Some sensitivities can be carried to absurdity. I have described before the apprentice piece, made in Europe by students after a number of years of study. The apprentice piece was usually a combination of everything that one had learned: as a rule it was a cabinet which was supposed to have as many working parts (drawers, doors, tambours) as possible. Often it was complicated in decoration as well; there would be veneering,

intarsia, or carving of some sort. These cabinets were showpieces. The crafts guild had a jury of master cabinetmakers who judged these pieces on the basis of strict rules. Certain things were important and others were not. Looking back, it seems to me that some of what was held *un*-important is—or should be—very important in the broad sense of the craft.

Part of the weakness of this judging process was that the piece was judged—one might say —on the basis of how it behaved on the Day of Judgment. The drawers, for instance, were supposed to work so perfectly that you could almost blow them in or out. As you opened one you felt the suction of air; as you pushed it in another swooshed out a bit, and when you closed a door its opposite tended to move out a little as they met.

These were beautifully made pieces, yes. But the tolerances here were not the tolerances of wood—they are more appropriate to metal, perhaps. Or plastics. If the jury was to come on Wednesday, and it rained on Monday or Tuesday, then the apprentice spent the entire night making minute adjustments of the drawers and other parts so they would work perfectly when the jury tried them. After the show, you put your pieces and the letters and various dignified documents that were in the cabinet up in the attic, because during the summer you could not move a drawer or open a door without a crowbar!

A true achievement is to make a fine cabinet—elegant, graceful, one with real character—and fit it with drawers and doors that work properly the year round. That requires skill rather than showmanship. There could be less veneer, and more use of solid wood. Everything could be done with a feeling for the material, for function, the work—and the moods of the seasons.

Another weakness of the traditional approach was—and in its echoes is—that the esthetic aspects were considered relatively unimportant. It did not matter whether the piece was of your own idea and design, or whether you had liked a drawing by a well-known designer and obtained permission to work from it. The accent was on technique, not esthetics.

Partly as a result of this we developed—and still support—craftsmen who are very proficient, but who have little or nothing to say that is their own. They are not artisans, but professional craftsmen whose work is a bit better though not really unlike that of small industry.

Some people talk about workmanship and of the few solid but sensitive objects they would like to live with just to contradict the tyranny of the Machine.

Where, I wonder, are those objects?

Certainly we are not producing them in Sweden today; not in wood we aren't: not after the somersault in our crafts education here. At our foremost school of fine and applied arts, where we really could have taken a positive step from dry tradition to know-how and a contemporary yet personal expression, we kicked over the traces some ten years ago. Threw out tradition *and* know-how, wiped everything out as far as cabinetmaking goes—and brought in Social Significance. Things for the many—the lowest common denominator in design and craft. Prototypes in chipboard, glue spilled on everything, the machines neglected, and people shuffling about looking sullen. Somebody setting up a huge dovetailing machine, and a fellow looking on says "Don't have it too tight—you've got to leave space for the glue, man!"

There are a few trade schools that teach the trade. If you want to work for the furniture industry that's the place to go.

What are the alternatives? When I'm feeling low, I really believe there are none. But then I meet some eager young person, someone who is a bit intimidated by the New Wave, but who also feels that it will wear itself out. We talk, and do what we can for one another. Amid our freedoms and aggressions and common denominator—we do have our little doubts. And hopes.

Meanwhile we wait. The apprentice system is gone in Sweden, as far as any renewed creativity is concerned; it is gone in most places. My former students write letters to the cabinetmakers' guilds in Denmark and elsewhere—and usually get no answer.

As yet no one here can clearly see beyond the wreckage of a fine craft, a pile-up of Tradition—and Survival.

Other places, other problems: in America and Canada it seems to be do-it-fast, make-it-big. Already in education the accent is on originality and on what I would call "muchness." The result are "statements" for better or for worse then. Often striking, heavy—and salable.

Is it so terribly difficult to teach a balance of feeling, true skill—and personal adventure? To abandon the criteria of quantity, at least for some, for a while? *Is* a single fine small thing less than two fair ones?

We have drifted into structured education and an idiom that is often a crafts mumble-jumble of sorts. The accepted and upgraded forms of expression are going to prove limited. Whole strata of woodcraft are missing, or much neglected. There is work waiting to be done that hasn't even been seriously attempted. Certain mild but difficult expressions of carving, for instance. Stacked pieces more finely balanced than those we are impressed by now. A modern intarsia, subtle, that with enough skill and inspiration might rise to a form of art; once we get away from flat surfaces and the present stiffness there would be many possibilities, including tactile ones. And we could do more to encourage refinement in contemporary furniture, pay more attention to the calm and the graceful that are satisfying without flash or pretence, because they have an identity of their own. As it is, we live with so much quasi-original. There is too little encouragement towards wholeness in our work.

The shortcomings need to be calmly observed and admitted

without animosity. Even then we'd have only a beginning: not enough, really, when we also need generosity and enthusiasm to achieve results in a softer light while being happy.

There is a reluctance to discuss these matters, a reluctance which in some places is by now a comfortable habit. Many of us craftsmen—and I mean us—are a bit on edge, or else aloof, when it comes to self-criticism. As workmen we have an excuse for a protective distance: as teachers or observers we have none.

Things seem so mixed up just now. The number of craftsmen is greatly increasing. Good; except that most of us are sort of milling, seeking a direction that's apt to be at odds with what we've been taught in school. What is coming? To what will we turn, now that the easy and the improvised are wearing thin? It is as if new possibilities were almost within reach. We chat sometimes, in schools, wonder about allowing a proper place in education for the Few alongside the Many. It's a real, disturbing matter: some have suffered from it, others evade it—and that, too, is disturbing.

One could, in generous moments, imagine a structured education (which we usually get) still flexible enough to allow for the Outsider without being condescending about it. Or intimidating these questioning people into the Survival pattern. In fact, we should be glad to have them with us. This is sometimes the case in smaller schools, though freedom there tends to be at the cost of real skill: it's usually either grass-rootsy or a kind of calculated art. As if we have to choose between being honestly clumsy or impressively slick.

There are discussions (often arguments) going on between those who claim that the process of doing is all-important—to the doer, that is—and those who say that what really matters is the result. I imagine, and like to believe, that if you get the doing right—I mean in the sense of what this book, and a lot more, is about—then the result rights itself to that. You do what you are. No more, no less. You develop, and your work develops: there's a play between doing things in a way that feels good— and getting good results. This truth is as old as the Greeks, probably older.

We've got to discover what feels good and is really good. We can isolate ourselves in the process, establish our own standards —even at the risk of self-delusion, maybe destruction. Or we can open up, question, and try another measure. What measure? Oh, that's the heart of it all! If I had to guess, and my life depended upon it, I'd say integrity. Not mine—something much more important, and durable. And because trying to define it, or explain, would be like trying to define Truth, I must give up and go back to my wood and my work.

Why is it so terribly difficult to achieve a balance between what is commonly called freedom —and the integrity of a disciplined medium?

Could it be that to find it we must ask more of ourselves as craftsmen?

There are too many questions: most of them will not be answered, though someone could try.

It would be sad if people find here a disturbing criticism or pessimism. Though it is true— when it comes to education, I am a pessimist. With this reservation: I would like nothing better than to be proved wrong.

I feel that in one or two places at least positive changes are occurring. There is a renewed interest in the subtleties of wood and tools and their use, and a desire to go with these beyond the romance of historical echoes or the limitations of mere competence—on to the satisfaction of knowing how to do a thing well, and experiencing the freedom that follows skill (not precedes—*follows*). Students begin by making fine classic tools, discover some of the richness of wood. Learn to see, and listen. And then do some thinking.

They just could be on the way to an insight which is the enjoyment of the simple at its best: refinement. To recognize it we must try to notice some of the subtleties along the way.

The ability to see. A truth from another kind of life: can we still use it?

I hope so. We are experiencing a paradox just now, a period when something neglected is waiting to be recognized—and to live anew by its serene presence in our cluttered midst.

2. WORKSHOP AND TOOLS

My workshop is in the half-basement of our little house, and consists of two rooms about sixteen by twenty-five feet each. In the one I have my machines, a workbench for some of the coarser and more dusty operations, and a part of the wood which I yet hope to use. There is space enough to band-saw planks I have brought home; most of them are short enough to be stood on end along one wall here. Others I must cross-cut first, which is always a worry because so much is at stake: there is something final about such a cut, and final can so easily mean fatal.

I have made three pairs of very light and strong T-type saw-horses of hardwood, with horizontal cross-pieces at various levels; I use these for sawing, sorting and sometimes stacking various small parts of whatever I am making.

The other room has more floor space. There is a fine old workbench at one end, with tool cabinets and a rack for clamps and other things. Along the other two available walls I keep horizontal stacks of wood, from the floor up. The little remaining wall space is taken up with racks for wood that has been re-sawn and is settling, so to speak, so that I can come to terms with it when we are both ready.

The wood I have here is heavy. Two- or three-inch-thick planks, flitches and quarters, nearly all of it hardwood and a lot of tropical varieties, varying in length from six to ten feet. Getting it in here from the delivery truck is a problem, though then I at least have some help. After which I am on my own. Year in and year out, moving these planks. No use saying I should stack them in the order I intend to use them—it doesn't work out. That's not how we live together. Some of them have been with me for nearly ten years, and still I don't know exactly what I will finally do with them. In fact, a few are so fine, so rare, so special to me that I am afraid to start that first cut. Other pieces come and go. It is a constant sorting and re-sorting, taking one more look, moving one piece to compare it with another, sawing to length, carrying wood that is heavy even in short lengths and holding it chest high while the band saw makes that first long, slow cut.

No, it is not an ideal situation, and I am not trying to present it as such. There are better places to locate a workshop. Better ways to store wood, and to solve the problem of having help when you need it.

But I believe many of us, while we are thinking about these things, want to start working. This is how one stubborn person did it. Looking back, I realize what an effort it has been. Fortunately, I was not completely aware of this earlier, or I might have given up, or changed my attitude, become more practical and less uncompromising.

I only sensed this then. I know it now.

In my little workshop I look around me at the neat stacks of wood and think of all the other fine wood that I have in piles stored at the company that supplies me with much of what I use. And I feel rich. So much beautiful wood!

Often I find myself thinking about one particular wood at a time; perhaps one family of wood at first, but soon it is one individual wood. I recall the differ-

Bench room of my workshop, with
wood being sorted.

Oak plank to be thought about, laid
out with an intention, sawn, and then
re-sawn. Note the cracks: one of them
is sixteen inches long.

ent planks I have, from parts of this country or from countries far away, and imagine what I might do with this one plank, or that one over there. Comparing them, I start wondering how they would go together as shades of the same color in a particular piece. I browse among planks I'd recognize in the dark, and discover again patterns I remember—and yet want to see once more.

Yes, I worry both the wood and myself.

I admit, too, that simply having this wood is exciting: a stimulating and encouraging feeling.

At the same time it can be distracting. You can get so engrossed in the search for wood, and with the wood you have, that you spend more time dreaming than you do working.

But I have worked because of the encouragement the wood itself gave me. At first it was only this: later on, the fine tools I made added to that encouragement.

I realize too, that there are completely different approaches to this problem of materials; some craftsmen reduce wood to an obedient material and devote all their energy to being original.

There are some very original people around these days, some of them talented and with the will to move mountains. But theirs is another way.

It is a question of making the best beginning you can. A beginning that will encourage you to continue. Being emotional about wood has helped me. I can get worked up about just one

plank and what I'm doing with it, and then do it, and I'm happy —if the work goes well.

The habit of acquiring wood is a good, expensive habit. I support it. Especially when you are young, because then you can—if you have the right friends, and suppliers who will cooperate with you—plan your search for different woods.

Besides, youth is part optimism: it may take a year or two to obtain some English brown oak, or Macassar ebony, or boxwood, or sandalwood; another year or more for that wood to finally dry—so what? When one is young, those years do not mean all that much. It's an adventure to go through the possibilities, to write letters and mail them to London, Hamburg, Bangkok, São Paolo—and wait for answers. The search can be difficult. Certainly success will be costly. Some of this we can adjust to our time and our means by working and living on a more modest scale. But maybe it is a bad sign when the urge to find more and better wood isn't there in us.

The physical task of handling wood is a part of our everyday life. A number of students I have met begin by setting up a workshop together with a friend, sharing the hard labor along with other things. There are also a few cooperative enterprises involving several craftsmen. This has its advantages and disadvantages. On the other hand, some of us are loners, and that's that. We will probably remain loners as long as our back holds up.

Going through a whole pile of

planks, some of them weighing two hundred pounds, I feel the strain. I feel alone, too—which is more than just strain.

If you are going to have a shop of your own and work by yourself, then as you accumulate wood, remember: provide as best you can for a sensible way of storing it! The ideal solution, where one can walk around and look at a plank and then pull it out with a minimum of effort, is to set up a rack or two with verticals of H- or T-shaped metal and a series of cleats protruding eighteen inches or so on each side. You want horizontal storage with side access to the wood. Easier said than done, what with the cost, and space; I know.

I myself have a very irrational way of handling my own wood: it is stacked all around me as it came to the shop, more or less by sorts, and aside from this there is little rhyme or reason to the order of the planks. Some wood is on end against the wall in the machine room. Sometimes I re-sort all or part of it, looking, looking. Maybe discovering some pieces I did not remember I had. Certainly getting tired. There is an awful lot of extra work connected with having a small workshop. But then—the place is cozy.

To those more sensible or more lucky I say: The more accessible your wood is, the better you will remember it. It's there, at hand, to prompt you whenever you run short of steam or new ideas.

Doing cabinetwork that involves many pieces of wood in each object you make—parts of drawers, door-frames, panels, and so on—you acquire a lot of leftover pieces, especially if you are cautious in your work.

Some of your scraps are very nice wood. In such cases it is good to have friends who make small things, do carving or jewelry boxes or whatnot, and to share this wood with them. I find myself giving a fair amount of wood away: not so much out of generosity; really, I am a miser when it comes to wood. I cling to these leftovers as long as I can, stuff them into corners of the shop or under my workbench. Until I am seized by a claustrophobic feeling of simply drowning, of being engulfed by all these scraps. Then I telephone someone and say "Come and get it, the garbage truck comes on Thursdays—you'd better be here before then!"

On Friday I will probably remember one of those little pieces of wood, and wish I still had it. As I sometimes say, "This stuff doesn't grow on trees, you know!"

Another person making mostly furniture might now and then have an urge to do a bit of woodturning, or to carve. It is good, sometimes, to take yourself away from the principal work that you are doing—from something complicated and strenuous which requires weeks or months of precise work—and for the sake of fun do a seemingly trivial object. I feel that way—though usually not until *after* I have finished something which took a lot of concentration. But then instead of making something sellable, I make planes, or

knives, or sharpen tools. By now it's a waste. I don't need more tools, and the ones I have are sharp.

Space—or lack of it—is one of the cabinetmaker's main problems. Especially when you are first setting up a workshop and have little or no margin to do with. You are living from day to day, perhaps borrowing money, hoping to get a larger shop later on. You crowd yourself into a small space and try to make the best of it.

Space is not only a matter of wood storage, machines and a good workbench, but also of habits. One fellow needs a room like a dancehall to do ordinary work in. Another chap has a Tom Thumb shop, a hole in the wall—and there he makes things that are bigger than the shop itself.

Some people can live and work in the midst of what I would call chaos. They would say it is a pleasant environment; an ordered chaos. Others are very meticulous in their work, they need to know where things are when they need them, they keep their workbench clean, their tools are in perfect order—for them, any other condition is incompatible with the work they do.

I have found that a neat and organized shop is very important to me. Much of the work I do, work that people enjoy to touch, is done with my planes and spokeshaves: it is the traces of a perfectly tuned tool on wood that is a joy. One doesn't leave tools like that in a heap on the bench.

I am tense if things aren't in order; I can't even *start*. I have a

complicated thing to put together; a lot of clamps, glue, rags, blocks and such—I want to be able to reach what I need when I need it. I'm gluing a joint, pushing the parts together (are they right-side-on?), I need a block between the clamp and a table-leg. I've got to have that block, I can't stand and frantically turn to look for a block that isn't there. If at that moment I pick up a clamp and it is clogged with glue—I say "if"; mine aren't—I might throw it through the window.

The process of gluing is a balancing act between self-control and hysterics. A week or two of work is at stake, and I can spoil the whole thing because I have ridiculously forgotten one lousy little detail of the act.

There is a great deal of method in the cabinetmaker's craft—if we want to admit it—logic and method, some of which goes back hundreds of years, that helps us even now to make and glue together a piece of furniture. We develop our own variations of that logic, modified and streamlined and so on. Still the process has to be lived through. And to make the best out of a method you need habits that correspond to the various steps of that method.

Long ago I used to sail in small boats. Mostly I sailed alone in an open boat on open water where it often blew hard. We had squalls and sudden storms, and I learned then that orderliness in a boat is the difference between safe enjoyment—and real trouble. You have all your lines neat and cleared in the cockpit, your sheets coiled properly; if there is a squall you can let go, and the line runs as it should. Whereas if you have a rat's-nest around your feet and the wind hits you, serious things happen. For me, sailing is a parallel to cabinet-making in the sense that there is a direct connection between certain habits and enjoyable results.

Years later I spent a good deal of time in the mountains, also there often alone on long journeys. And there too the way you think through the things you are going to have with you, the way you pack them, protect them against bad weather—determines whether you are going to be warm and dry and comfortable in a rainstorm, or soaked and miserable and grouchy.

Some of us have a need for orderliness, whatever it may cost us in the way of unnecessary worrying and fretting. A friend of mine is a wonderful guitar builder. His habits are almost the opposite of mine. If you look at his workbench, you will wonder how in the world anyone can ever work there. Yet he makes these world-famous guitars, coveted instruments. He simply lets the chaos accumulate in his shop while he is going through the whole process of building a guitar, and out of disorder grows this classic instrument. I do not know whether he leaves one mess and moves on to the next guitar—and another mess—but I think he does some half-hearted cleaning up somewhere along the way. At any rate, the relationship between the superb work he does and the state of his shop is a valid contradiction to all that I preach about orderliness.

MACHINES

The few persons who have spent some time puttering in my workshop have said nice things about it. And since I am often asked what kind of a shop I think is ideal, which machines are best, or most important, I will dwell a little on these matters.

If you want to know how to set up a shop or what the ideal shop is, all I can say is: The best shop for you is the one in which you can do good work and feel happy doing it. *Balancing your environment in a way that gives you harmony is all-important.* You do not necessarily need plenty of room and costly equipment. But it must be a place where you feel good and where you can work in your own way, with wood that interests you, making the things you feel are in you, the experiences they represent. The work matters, not the reward in terms of survival or praise, though praise can be nice, too. You must not be intimidated by your surroundings, pushed into what I'd call "pro" thinking and doing. Don't let your education, friends, advisers tell you that you've got to be able to turn the stuff out—whatever that means. Usually it means you should think and work competitively—on the same basic terms as the craftsmen around you. If this is what you want, then get that belt sander, and disc-type sander, too, and some of the other equipment whose primary purpose is to save sweat. If you are the sort of person who wants the result of your efforts to be as personal as the way you feel about making your pieces, there is another point to start from.

So for what it's worth, I'll tell you what I have to work with. First, a beautiful little eighteen-inch band saw. I say "little" because it is so compact, so simple. Cast-iron frame, nicely balanced wheels which I clean dutifully with a suede brush often enough to keep them from becoming clogged and uneven. Bakelite guides: these I true with a file now and then. Behind the guides are the usual pressure wheels—mine run simply in brass bushings. Band-saw blades, and how I use my saw, are discussed elsewhere in this book, but I repeat here: thick, heavy-duty blades are not the secret to good sawing—they throb and weave and strain the whole works without good reason. For a six- or eight-inch cut in hardwood, a 3/8- or 1/2-inch blade is actually better. The secret of a fine cut—if it is a secret—is a good saw, a sharp blade of the right sort, and a bit of skill, patience, and a certain touch—even on a machine. Of all my machines, the band saw has done the most to help me use wood the way I really want to.

The jointer I have serves also as a thicknesser—though it is not the usual over-under type. It has a post and adjustable plate of cast iron on a wheel screw: with this set to the desired thickness you simply drop

Eighteen-inch bandsaw as described in
text. The vacuum cleaner collects most
of the dust.

Band-sawed "veneer" from the same
plank as the rest of the cabinet. The
thickness (about 3/32 inch) allows for
some polishing, planing, etc. and finish
in the same way as solid wood. Such
sawn-veneer surfaces, when properly
glued on a block heart, remain constant and unmoving—thus allowing for
more subtle constructions than with
solid wood throughout. A not too
difficult but much neglected part of
the cabinetmaker's repertoire.

the feed half of the table, snap into place a spring which pushes the work up against the plate, adjust the tension with the feed table—and you're ready to go.

There is no self-feed; you push the pieces through by hand. No good? Too much work? Those who have used this machine like it. As to work: you are not apt to have the sort of equipment for doing production things or stacked pieces or the like. For one-man cabinetmaking it is fine, cuts cleanly and evenly: if you set it right you can run a piece fast or slow, straight on, or at a diagonal if the grain is tricky. It takes thicknesses from six inches to 1/8 inch or even less; there being no rollers, the pieces aren't under strain as they come through. The two cutters (knives) are only eight inches wide, which is a pity, since I work mainly with surfaces. As it is, I have to re-saw and joint some of these an extra time.

The knives I use now are cobalt-edged. I had the high-speed steel ones at first, and still think they cut cleaner on some of the softer woods. But only when they are very sharp, which is not for long, unless you want to be a slave to them. Since I hand-plane all surfaces and joints anyway, the cobalt knives make more sense here.

The machine could be wider, though then it would be another machine. As it is, it is good: solid, dependable, and compact. Together with the band saw it has served me faithfully for twenty years. Both these machines are now out of date, that

is to say, out of production, which is regrettable. Friends from abroad have tried to buy them, and I have promised them when my time is up. These machines will outlast me, that's for sure.

For a while, when I first started, I could not afford a table saw. This forced me to simplify parts of my work almost beyond what I felt was reasonable, and as soon as I could I bought a very small six-inch Ulmia bench-model saw. I mounted it on a wood stand (of real Andaman padouk it was: I had lots of padouk then, whereas now every sliver of it is precious), and for a year or two this was my table saw. I was obliged to keep certain of my work within range of this saw, but now I could at least do smaller joints more easily.

My horizontal mortiser at this time was makeshift, nothing more than a 3/8-inch portable electric drill mounted on a wooden block by two yokes with wing-nuts. I could clamp this setup on my workbench: together with a right-angle plywood "table" held in the bench vise, it served to make simple mortises. Someone may be surprised at my not mentioning the slot mortisers so common in American woodshops; I know about these. They are by intent an industrial machine, for quick results; they produce straight-edged mortises (often with a smell of burnt wood), hardly the carefully cut ones with rounded corners to which I am accustomed. The horizontal mortiser is a much used machine in Eu-

rope, and I believe it will in time be, in its simpler form, accepted by conscientious craftsmen everywhere.

I had a large Stanley router, and made a floor-type wood stand for it, again with a wood yoke and wing-nut to hold the machine. The table was a cast-iron band-saw table, its small opening centered on the router. This worked rather well, though I was limited to the bits which fitted the machine.

I learned some things during this time when some of my machines verged on being inadequate. Probably this was when I began to realize that much of the work I most wanted to do did not stem from my having certain machines. When the equipment I had could help me I worked and was less tired—when it could not, I worked and was very, very tired. But I did get things done. There was something of the struggle in the results: a closeness to the way I had worked by hand, the absence of any final mechanical influence. The pieces weren't primitive because of the way the shop was equipped—it's just that they might have been finished a bit sooner. I learned more then than at any time before or since. Looking at a piece made during that period of discovery I wonder: how did I manage to do it?

I do not think I would recommend this sort of struggle to others. Or do I hear volunteers?

After a while I was able to get the table saw I have now, a ten-inch Swedish one, very sturdy and simple without being crude. The belt-driven arbor

Ten-inch jointer-planer in my workshop.

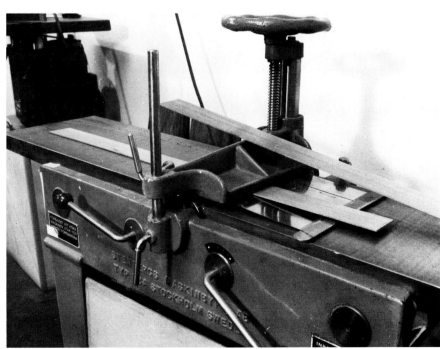

which takes the saw-blade at one end has a chuck at the other, and under this chuck is a steady rest; together these make a simplified horizontal mortiser, the only one I have, and quite satisfactory. The chuck is raised and positioned by the same lever that raises and lowers the saw blade, there is a fine adjustment which serves both chuck and saw, so one can work with great accuracy. The sturdy fence has a micro-screw as well, the whole machine in all its simplicity is completely logical: no fuss, no frills. Also no tinny parts or do-it-all-for-you finesses. There may be other saws as good as this one, or better, but I wouldn't bet on it.

Granted, I wouldn't mind having a tilting arbor saw (on mine, the table itself tilts, and only one way). But then I would have to get a horizontal mortiser as a separate machine: more ex-

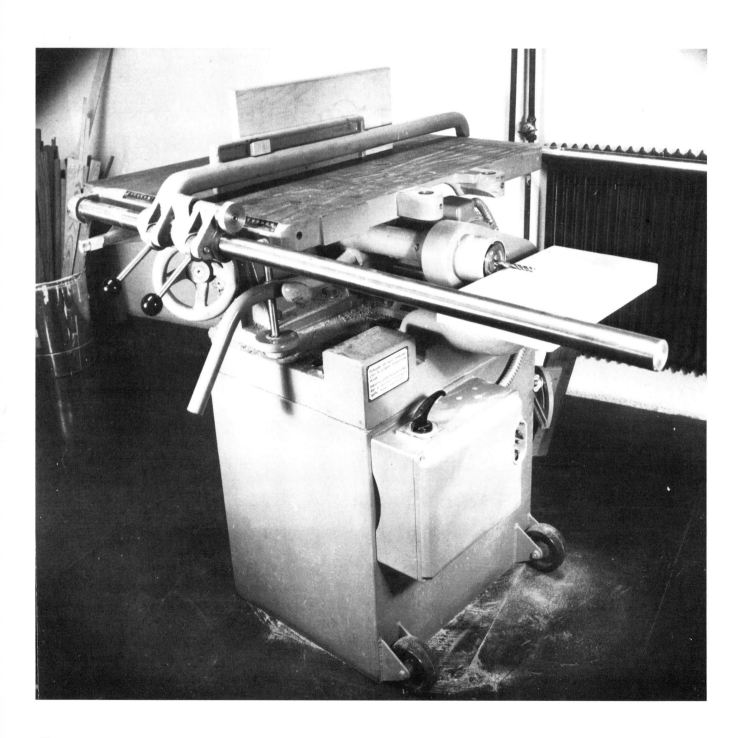

My table saw. Having the chuck on the same arbor as the saw-blade makes a suitable horizontal mortiser when it is used with steady rest (as here).

pense, more floor space. Since I work alone, doing one operation at a time, it is more important that my machines do clean, accurate work than that they save time or have a larger capacity than I can make use of.

The Stanley router as I had it mounted served me as a shaper for several years, while I saved, and looked for another one. During this time I visited schools in Sweden and in America, saw different shapers—and concluded that most of them were too large for the work they were asked to do. A big shaper is not only expensive, but also a very frightening invention: even the medium-sized ones are scary. I hardly ever see anyone using them without being tense. Besides, their use is limited to the standard cutters they take.

When it comes to small crisp work—as it often does—we use a hand-router. But here, too, we have less than an ideal situation: the machine screeches, there is a lot of vibration, the guides are not as steady as they might be. At one school we hung our router under a plywood table clamped to a bench—this was an improvement, but hardly the solid, smooth-running and yet versatile solution I felt was possible.

Finally, I found it. An Italian machine with a sixteen-inch-square cast-iron table, simple two-post height adjustment, and belt drive. At once I liked the way it sounded; I could hold my hand on the table and hardly feel any vibration as I listened to that smooth, steady sound of twelve thousand RPM.

I didn't only fall for the sweet sound of that shaper; it had other good qualities: compact size and reasonable price among them. It came with a spindle intended for grooved washers with paired slide-in cutters. The first thing I did was to take it to a machine shop where they remodeled the shaft and threaded it for a beautiful Bofors chuck with interchangeable cones (collets) that would enable me to use a wide variety of bits and cutters, from European standards to the 1/4-inch-shank Stanley series. When it comes to shapers, I can say that a solution which allows the use of widely different bits and cutters is a good one.

So now I have the shaper which suits me best—one on which I can do anything from the usual table or chair and cabinetwork to the smallest details in a jewelry box or other tiny piece. Doing such work, it is important to keep the tools absolutely sharp and clean—the work itself comes easier if you *use the machine with a light touch. Feed slowly. Better two thin cuts than one that is forced.* With a bit of inventiveness you can set up your work using a rest and stops right for the occasion, so as to almost eliminate the possibility of errors. *Be*

neither afraid of your machine, nor nonchalant towards it, but respect it and use it accordingly.

For overhead routing and the few occasions when I use a template I have a Black & Decker hand-router. Together with a 3/8-inch portable electric drill, this completes my mechanical equipment.

My machines are not at all extraordinary, though they are good for the work I do. One can find similar machines in almost any part of the world. Some tools are very specific: one can recommend a size, shape, or weight together with a manufacturer. Machines are more involved: which is why I leave you with only an idea of how some of them relate to a certain type of work.

It is mostly a matter of determination. And of means, though I sincerely hope they won't keep you from arriving at the point where you can judge the balance you want between the work you hope to do—and the extent to which you will allow your machines to leave their mark upon that work.

At an early stage, when we do not as yet know our strengths and weaknesses, it is easy to succumb to temptations. Schools don't always prepare us to make the right decisions. Whether schools are over-equipped and their do-it-the-easiest-way attitude comes from this, or whether the educational attitude itself leads to an abundance of sanders and such—at the price of better hand-tools, true skill, and more individual results—I can't say. Some educators do not

seem to be aware of the *content* of cabinetmaking, which for many of us is its most satisfying part. Ours is a complex craft, and it is easy to imagine, at the distance some choose to keep, that machines are an answer to the complexity. Maybe. As a general solution, yes. But there is another level, another attitude, another kind of satisfaction: namely the sensitivity which is the basis of real skill. And I do not see how anyone can sell self-expression and the need for emotional satisfaction—and still be unaware of that sensitivity with the possibilities it affords. It's as if the aim were to provide for survival rather than happiness.

Some will claim that the one precludes the other. And others will answer: not at any price, it doesn't.

As we work with our machines, we develop habits. After working for years alone in my shop, I am like the ship's engineer: he is most apt to notice his engines when they miss a beat. I find myself using a machine, holding pieces of wood a certain way, feeding them through, putting them aside—while thinking, at least in part, about something else. This is not good. Though since I have been fortunate enough not to have accidents it does confirm that somewhere early I formed a few commonsense habits. I don't use my table saw unless I have to: that is, I do not re-saw on it, or rip anything large; in fact I haven't even a blade for such work. Mostly I square off various pieces, and do joints. A few drawer sides and the like I cut to

Shaper-router (an Italian model available in U.S.). The wood stand is home-made, but a metal one can be ordered with the machine.

Same machine showing chuck and interchangeable collets to take various types of standard cutters, including popular series with ¼-inch shank.

width; for this I clamp a long piece onto my permanent fence—which is fairly short, and high enough for doing all the work I need with various joints. When cutting these joints I feed each piece evenly—not slow, not fast—and keep several fingers of my left hand—the one doing most of the holding, down low—curled over the top edge of the fence. With the saw-blade very sharp and clean, and the fence exactly parallel to the blade, I get good smooth cuts without being tense about the work—even though I dislike the very nature of a table saw intensely.

Table-saw in use. Develop the habit of caution but not undue fear.

My jointer has a primitive guard on a bar which can be raised or lowered. No springs, no pivot. And because it is so simple I actually do use it, since it does not irritate me or interfere with the work. Part of the problem around safety measures—all sorts of attachments on various machines—is that while they are theoretically right, and even definitely so in a production setup—they are a nuisance to a certain kind of craftsman, and are apt to be removed, or swung to one side. *Now, I am not advocating doing this*, but only reminding myself that for me the forming of very cautious habits has been the best possible insurance against accidents.

However, even some good habits carry risks: The only time I have had a mishap was soon after I got the Stanley router and mounted it under the table. Earlier I had used another model router, with its starting switch placed differently. Now, with the big Stanley I was changing a bit, more or less doing it the way I'd done before—when I tripped the switch. My left hand was still lingering near the tool it had just pushed into place—and I nicked a finger-tip.

Aside from this, I have been lucky all these years, not only with machines but also with the many hand-type cutting tools I use so much. Maybe this is simply luck, though I like to think it is also because I keep these tools in such fine order that I do not have to force them to do anything—and they in turn don't need to bite back at me.

Jointer and simple guard.

73

WORKBENCHES

With a few forgivable exceptions, the most important part of a cabinetmaker's shop is his workbench. If our shop is where we live, then our workbench is where we think and feel, where we do what is most satisfying to us as craftsmen.

A classic—or call it traditional—cabinetmaker's workbench is a fine piece of equipment. Having seen benches here and there, in good hands and bad, let me add this: how we use our bench, and care for it, determines how good or bad it really is. And this in turn influences our work. We plane surfaces flat, joint pieces by planing edges absolutely straight—and *this we cannot do on a workbench which has a dip, or wind, or is otherwise out of true.*

I once attended a school where some workbenches in use were more than eighty years old. The experienced eye noticed that the tops of these benches were a bit thinner than when new, and there were some other signs of honest wear, but in terms of their usability, these veteran benches were just fine. Maybe they were originally better than some of the ones we get nowadays: somebody took the time to choose the wood and season it well, the wood screws for the vises were turned to last a lifetime, the stand was sturdily through-jointed and held with wooden wedges. The benches were well made, and deserved the good care which they usually received. It was considered an honor to be allotted one of them:

you were one of many craftsmen-to-be whom it had served, and after you there would be others. So we kept up a kind of style, there were dos and don'ts, and fellows keeping a comradely but strict eye on one another.

You did not spill glue on your bench, or if you were awkward enough to do so, you cleaned it up right away.

You did not damage your bench with cutting tools: nobody with self-respect would cut joints directly on its surface, or drill through something placed there. Fresh nicks on one of these old benches were cause for shame.

You did not neglect the bench vises, and let them get sloppy. The main vise with its sliding section cut for several stops and the short L-shaped outer part that took the wooden screw-head was a fairly complex thing. It ran on hardwood strips fitted underneath, these wore away in time and needed adjusting or to be replaced—otherwise the whole part sagged below the level of the rest of the bench.

You did not leave your bench at the end of the day with its vise wide open, or "jawning," as we used to say. Partly this was considered bad manners; also, anyone who has bumped at full walking speed into a vise left so the screws with their pins stick out into the aisle knows how and where it hits you.

Since the whole bench was made of wood, there was a certain normal mid-season tolerance to be observed—a state in which all parts worked properly at any time of the year.

First and last, *you treated your workbench with respect.* Cleaned it with the help of a cabinetmaker's scraper. Checked it now and then for wind or a dip, and corrected any such fault with a few cautious cuts using a large jointer plane. This is not as simple as it sounds; it requires a good eye and a portion of patience.

Sometimes, when the teacher came by and we discussed something, we'd whip out a pencil and draw a diagram on the benchtop. Afterwards we erased it, maybe finishing off the incident with a few strokes of our scraper.

Once a year we had a general cleanup that included our benches. Amid a cloud of dust, piles of junk were dumped from all sorts of storage places under each bench; the drawer, secret pockets tucked under the top itself; the space between the stretchers might yield anything from half-eaten sandwiches to carefully hoarded bits of very rare wood. We cleaned the benchtop and trough, checked the vises, tightened wedges. Some of us treated the surfaces with boiled linseed oil, others left the newly scraped beechwood as it was—this being a sign we intended to keep it that way, clean and bright.

Mind now, this was not a very strict school with all sorts of rules; the place was friendly and had a rather free-and-easy air about it. What kept things from deteriorating was not fear of the devil, but a certain amount of knowledge and feeling for a craft that went way, way back to before those benches—and would go far, far beyond them and us and those after us who would one day stand here working. So what we felt, if it wasn't reverence, was at least a genuine respect for the place, a feeling helped along by certain tangible things such as work done better because of not having to fight the bench while using it.

Get (or make) *a really good workbench.* It will be about seven feet long (2.20 meters) and cost a mint, but do get it nonetheless. The once wooden visescrews are now of steel, the stretchers are bolted in place, the stand on the Swedish and perhaps even the Danish models are of somewhat inferior-grade fir—aside from these details, it's the same traditional bench, only minus a bit of romance.

The workbenches we can buy today are not inferior to those we had in the good old days. The best model made by Ulmia is indeed fine. So are the ones from the reputable firms in Sweden and Denmark—once you separate the true cabinetmaker's bench—full size and with its hardwood (usually beech) top about four inches thick—from the smaller and often flimsy hobby-size models.

I read an article not long ago by someone who supposedly "designed" a cabinetmaker's workbench. Seeing the drawing, and the result, I had to conclude to myself that this was simply the classic Danish *snickarbänk*, which never was designed, but rather *evolved* through generations of use: trial, error, attempted small changes—all within the bounds of the basic usage of such a workbench. As it stands now it is a fine example of design *from within*, a craftsman's piece too good to need a name. If you make one, be sure you can make it as good as it deserves to be.

A workbench like this contains a lot of wood. No matter what the advertisements say, such a wooden object is not the stable, guaranteed one-hundred-percent non-warp surface some of us hope for. *It has, or will develop, a temperament of its own.* It will move a little, warp or wind or simply shrink and maybe crack here and there along a glue-joint. *Be patient with it.* Use it for half a year or so; observe how it reacts to the conditions of your workshop. Choose an in-between season when the air is neither very dry nor very humid, and, if need be, true the surfaces carefully—seeing at first that the bench rests well on the floor. Never mind all that shiny varnish; it should not have been there in the first place; nothing is better than a cleanly scraped bench-top, lightly oiled at most. Wedges on the stretchers have been replaced by bolts, on some benches the bolt-head nearest the main vise may interfere with a long piece held protruding straight down from the vise: if so, you'll need to countersink the bolt.

Make a storage space of the section between the stretchers—but simple, not an invitation to a hoarder's nest: just a bottom of slats and a removable top of some sort, a piece of plywood or chipboard will do.

The main or right-end vise might not be absolutely true; in fact, it seldom is perfect, even on a new bench. Spend whatever time you must in order to first line it up and then get its two jaw surfaces parallel and flat. Be critical about this: you won't regret it.

The vises are for firmly holding a piece of wood while we work it, not for cracking nuts. On a fine bench either of the two vises will take a piece three inches thick or a tenth of that, just a thin bit of veneer, and hold it properly so that it will not pivot under the pressure of a tool, or give way at one end as you saw or chisel it. We are sometimes urged to use the opening at the far side of the right-end vise, formed by the "L" of its corner point. I have seen this done at schools. But never by a conscientious cabinetmaker using *his own* bench. Because sooner or later such usage will overstrain that corner point: the plain logic of the vise construction is against pressure at the tip of that L-shaped piece. Your classic bench has *two* vises. Not three. These vises will have their jaws flat and clean, and free from nicks. The jaws may be lined with hard but thin Masonite neatly trimmed and trued. The vise closes so that it will hold a single sheet of paper.

One of the first things those of us who pamper our tools do is to put aside (I'm tempted to say throw away) the steel bench stops—and make new ones of hardwood. Somebody may not approve, I know, but for one reason or another those who have made and started to use wooden bench stops have kept

on using these. They'll break? Well, yes: if you are big and strong and brace yourself against the wall and give the screw all you've got—they are apt to break. But then, so is the piece of wood between them! Force may be essential at times with pieces in the vise itself: with stops it is often a waste, since these are only a part of what holds the work in place; if you use them properly, the main load is on the bench top itself. I have several pairs of stops made of hornbeam, patterned after the original steel ones, with a small spring set in behind the thin wood clip which is screwed to the stop at the down end. I've been using these for years, and no longer remember how it feels to run into a steel stop with a chisel or a plane: the damage, the irritation, the time lost are best forgotten. Oh, yes, we do set those stops low, and allow for wood to be cut away: which makes it all the more strange when we still do run into them.

For me, the classical cabinet-maker's workbench with its subtle system of stops is ideal: I can't quite accept any other. At a school in Canada I saw benches of two-inch-thick hardwood, the top unbroken, lockers under, and pivot-type vises at opposite corners. The vises were excellent, and maybe if one used them long enough one would not

Main or right-hand vise of thirty-year-old workbench. Jaws lined with ¼-inch Masonite are easily trued. A softer material (such as Treetex or felt) is less suitable as lining.

miss the table surface as a rest, and those adjustable stops, though I doubt it.

Part of the reason for my devoting so much attention to the workbench is that it in turn affects the way some of us use our tools. It's a nice place to work, and tools like it as a resting-place. Still: it is a pity to hide that fine beechwood surface under a pile of tools—a fact which encourages us to put away tools we aren't using at the moment. *One of the worst dangers to a sharp tool is another tool left close by:* it is surprising how easily a sharp edge can be nicked, or the teeth on a saw bent, while we move a tool along our bench, looking among other tools for something as innocent and elusive as a pencil.

Without being impractical about it, I have tried to reduce the number of metal things around me. This is a matter of personal feeling I wouldn't impose on others, but for those who care: it is pleasant to have squares and diagonal sticks made of wood. Such friendly aids are easy to make, and serve their purpose very well. The squares need not be graduated, since most of us prefer a rule for measuring—a square being awkward for this purpose. Wood squares, made with care, are as accurate as any square need be, and certainly more pleasing to use than metal ones.

Diagonal measuring sticks belong to the tradition of our craft; with them one can check the alignment of a cabinet-case or drawer more accurately than any other way. The two sticks of about equal length are held together with a pair of wooden collars in a snug sliding fit. It is customary to fasten the collars about six inches apart near the middle of one stick. The tops of each stick should be neatly beveled at about forty-five degrees both ways. A suitable length (closed) for ordinary cabinetmaking might be thirty inches; for smaller work the sticks can be twelve inches long or even less, according to need.

Bench-stops of wood (hornbeam) with spring from ball-point pen.

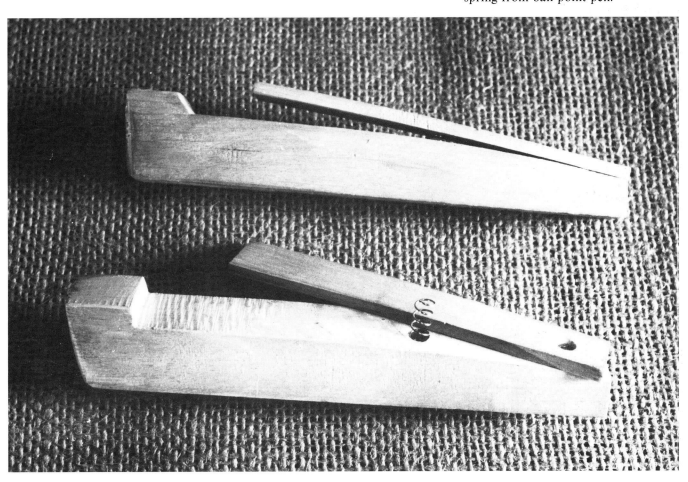

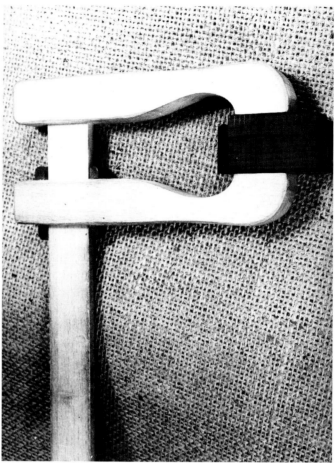

Clamps made of beechwood. Wedges slope so as to create pressure as movable jaw is pushed down at back. Jaws can be lined with leather. Pin (piece of dowel) near end of bar serves as stop.

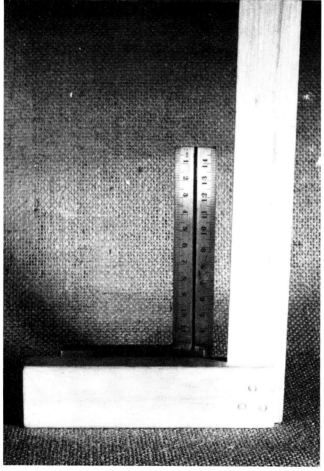

Square made of hornbeam.

→

Diagonal sticks. The most reliable way of checking for squareness in a cabinet case, box, drawer, etc. Sticks of wood, collars of wood, Teflon, or Bakelite.

Lighting is another element to be discussed when we talk about our workbench and tools. Wood makes its own special demands as to light: it is a very subtle—I will say evasive—material in its various qualities. Unless we have the proper light and use it sensitively, we can be easily fooled in our self-confidence at work—only to be reminded of this, too late, by sunlight on the finished piece. A room might be pleasant, and full of light, and yet as far as discovering details in wood goes, the lighting is wrong. The angle at which the light comes is vital: we need to be able to vary this: low to catch a slight unevenness of surface, at another angle to follow a rounded edge or a bevel, this way and that when doing dovetails and other minute work. We want warm light with an undertone of sunshine, light that will not tire us, or distort the true colors and texture of the wood we are using.

The matter of warmth is obviously more than one of light, or a fine, well-kept bench: it is the mood of the place where we spend so much of our time and efforts. That mood is important. Even when we are seemingly lost in our work, oblivious of all else, it is there, affecting us. This is perhaps why some schools seem more sympathetic than others. The buildings may be great, the reputation impressive, the staff capable; but unless there is a certain feeling about the shop itself, a lived-in sense—not necessarily romantic or picturesque, but friendly—then we are not quite at home there, not at ease. A school may start with all sorts of ambitions and resources—but if there isn't a warmth about the place, or at least the awareness of warmth and human touches soon to come, there will be no harmony. Difficult people, craftsmen.

In our own workshop we can usually create the mood that suits us, even if it takes time to reveal its importance. Most of us need a place which invites us to stay and work. But I sometimes wonder: what is home, what is happiness in our work? I stand here in my cozy shop, at my workbench with my wood, tools, ideas, the warm feel of the work itself, and all is as it should be. For a day, a week, a month it is so—until something inside me begins to stir. It is as if I were expecting someone to come, something to happen. A face at the window, a knock on the door. A visitor, a friendly voice. I work alone, happy at my work, harmonious—until the time when I want to hear once more the answer: For whom?

In a sense, work is happiness only when it takes us to those who also care.

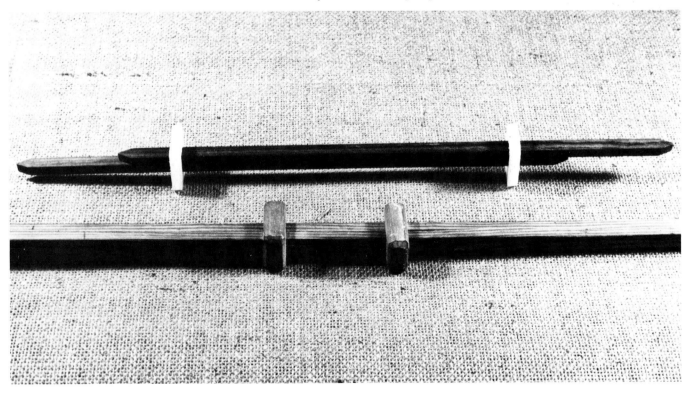

PLANES

Following is a step-by-step description of how to make a cabinetmaker's plane. It is not an anybody-can-do-it kind of thing. I have assumed that you have worked a bit with wood, and used the various planes available on the market, and are not quite satisfied with these. Or simply are curious as to how enjoyable and gratifying working with a fine plane can become.

First there is the matter of irons. There are primarily three types being made today; the ones for various standard iron planes, those for wooden planes—and, lastly, irons for low-angle block planes. The first two are long, and these we will shorten. The ones for wooden planes have a breaker of the sort we can use: for the others we will make our own breakers.

Irons for metal planes have the chip breaker and its screw high up; both iron and breaker are long. This results in a "high" plane; I mean it comes up high off the work. It is usually fitted with a handle or grip, and a knob. You can use it in only one position, really; its construction presupposes this is the way you want to hold it and use it. This may or may not be the case.

The second kind of iron is—or was originally—for the classic wooden plane, let's call it the old-fashioned one. This iron too is long but its breaker is fairly short, and the screw is far down; also, the breaker rounds off towards the iron in a way different from that for metal planes. These irons can be the old-style thick ones or they may be as thin as those for metal planes, or something in between: it doesn't matter, as long as the steel is of good, smooth quality. Some say that thick irons result in better planes. Well, they don't—not if the plane is otherwise properly made, with the iron making perfect contact at the base of the slope where it leaves the plane. Thick irons or thin, the important thing is to have them short—and with a breaker that fits. We want a low, snug plane which is essentially different from the ones, metal or wood, that are commonly available.

Standard iron plane and wood plane as described in text.

Plane-irons. At left, iron for common metal plane. Middle: long plane iron (either for metal or for wood plane) cut down for use in wood plane as described in text. Right: block-plane iron with slot lengthened.

As to widths: there is a 1 5/8- and a 1 3/4-inch iron widely sold, usually either for a wood or a metal plane. These are long irons, and if you leave them as they are they will protrude up disturbingly from the plane; one of the main advantages of the plane we are making is that we will be free to hold it in any number of ways, including putting your whole hand up over the back of it to get a firm hold and more even pressure as you work, without chafing against the iron. An iron about 4 1/2 inches long will be about right: long enough to tap into position, but not so long as to be irritating when you use the plane. Hacksaw it down to just under 4 1/2 inches and then round the ends carefully. Don't let the two prongs left when you have sawn through the slot bother you; this is no disadvantage. Just round them nicely. Later you will find that the breaker with its screw is easier to slide on and off because the slot is open on these cut-down irons. Standard block-plane irons are 1 3/8 and 1 5/8 inches wide; these are of a handy size and have the upper end nicely rounded, which is an additional comfort. If need be, you can lengthen the slot in them with the aid of a hacksaw. All these irons are good widths, the narrower one making a small, very handy little plane about six inches long, the other an inter-

Typical breakers for plane-irons. The left one is for metal planes. At right, one suitable for a wood plane of the type described in the text. Note difference in length and distance to set-screw.

81

mediate size for an all-round plane ten or eleven inches long, and the 1 3/4-inch width suitable for a fairly large plane some eighteen inches long, though not much more. I wouldn't go wider than 1 3/4 inches because very wide irons make for a rather awkward plane, difficult to hold comfortably.

If you can't find suitable breakers, it is not difficult to make them. Simply obtain some mild steel (or even iron) the same width as the plane irons you have, and make the breaker as the sketch and photo show. Keep the edges straight and the angles true. Bend one end so the breaker will lift from the iron about 1/16 inch, drill and tap a hole

for the screw at a point that fits the opening in the iron you have, file or grind a nice rounded taper along the lower edge of the breaker, and see that it meets the iron in a line that is absolutely tight farthest out. The way this part of the breaker curves down and meets the iron, how neat and polished it is just here—is most important. Never underestimate the role of each of these details concerning the breaker.

The plane body itself should be of hard and fairly heavy wood, though not unpleasant or too difficult to work. Hornbeam is good, also hard maple, close-grained oak, perhaps doussie, or one of the fruit-tree

woods such as pear or apple. It will be necessary to put a separate shoe, or make an insert of very hard wood such as secupira or ironbark on all but the hardest of these. With hornbeam and similar woods one can make the entire plane out of the same stock.

Our method could be described as a "sandwich," the body of the plane being sawn (and later re-assembled) into three lengthwise sections. The main part (center section) should be about 1/16 inch wider than the iron you have selected: the two outer sections, the thin "slabs," are usually 3/8 or 7/16 inch thick to begin with. Keep the pieces two or three inches

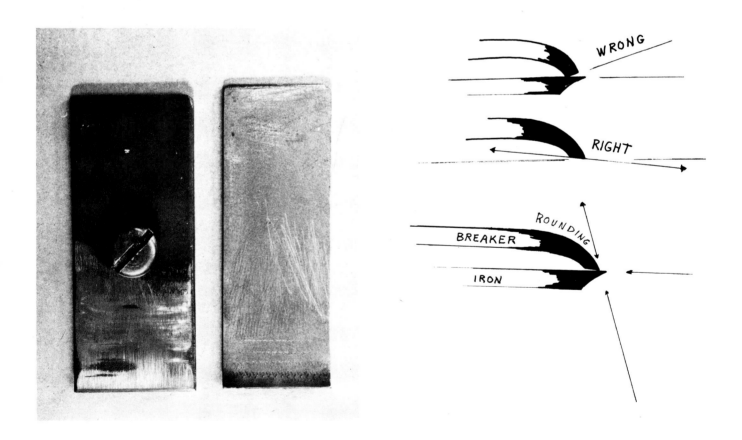

longer than the size of your finished plane. The height I have been using is about 2 1/2 inches, which has proved adequate for both short and long planes. We saw the stock carefully lengthwise and mark the parts so as to be able to put them together in the same order later on. Smooth the surfaces that are going to be glued—especially those of the center section. This is important, since you will be cutting this thicker part into two short pieces—and these must be of equal thickness when gluing. Watch out, or you will have trouble trying to true them up later.

Band-sawing stock for wood plane.

Laying out for width of center part of the plane.

The angle of the iron, the planing angle, is about forty-five degrees. I have used forty-two- to forty-three-degree angles on many of my planes, experimented with "steep" planes (forty-seven to fifty degrees)—and returned to forty-five degrees. The steep ones grip the work well, but they tend to dig or scrape a little.

After you have cut and smoothed the pieces, saw the sloping parts of the mid-section. The forward one can be about fifteen degrees—so as to enable you to clear the shavings if they pile up when you are doing heavy work.

Place the two mid-pieces and the iron on your workbench, and arrange these so that the iron does not quite protrude through the opening at the bottom. Note this carefully: if the plane is not to have a separate shoe added on, the iron should touch the front slope just above the front edge of the opening.

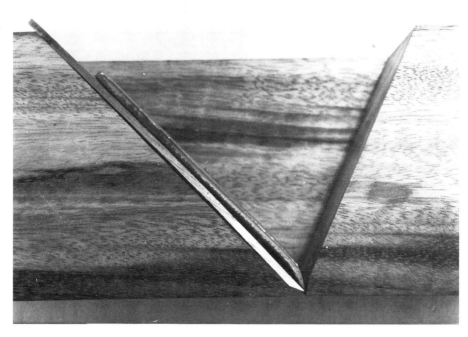

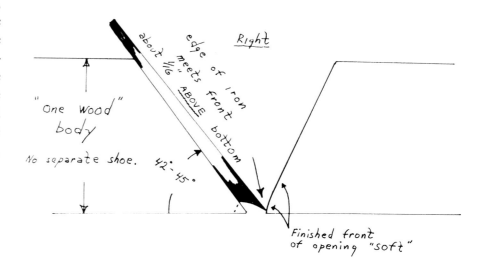

Position of iron and breaker for plane *without* separate shoe. Note gently decreasing slope of front edge of opening: this is important, as it prevents the very thin (final) opening in the finished plane from increasing too rapidly as the plane-bottom wears.

84

However, if you are going to add a hardwood shoe, then make the opening at this point larger to allow for the additional thickness of the shoe, which will be about 3/8 inch. It is important to decide early whether or not you are going to add a shoe. When you have determined this, and the sloping parts are right in position, clamp them firmly between the sides and then locate them with dowels so they will remain in place whenever you put the parts of your plane together as you proceed.

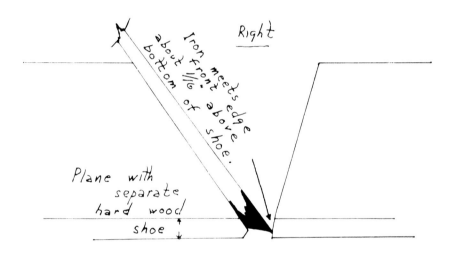

Positioning iron and breaker for plane with separate hardwood shoe. (The shoe is about ⅜ inch thick finished.)

Make the recess for the breaker-screw, since you will now determine where the cross-pin will be that holds the wedge; for this you need the iron *and* breaker in position. Allow 3/16 inch or so for that wooden wedge, mark for the hole—3/8 inch will do—and drill it very carefully at right angles to the sides, straight across the opening. Keep this hole rather low on the body of the plane, say 1 1/4″ up from the bottom. Placing it higher will probably interfere with the final shape of your

Drilling for dowels to hold parts of plane in position for further layout and then gluing.

Recess for screw-head on underside of breaker.

plane, which usually dips along the middle area.

Make the cross-pin—in fact, make several, because it is so easy to spoil one. Have it square or rectangular first and saw the tenons square, then round these to fit the hole. Shape the pin nicely. It should be a snug fit, though not too tight, since this pin moves slightly to follow the exact slope of the wedge. Set in the cross-pin, put the plane together with the iron and breaker in place, maybe make a trial wedge to check that everything fits and is right on; the pin should be parallel with the iron and breaker—you don't want to have to make a lopsided final wedge to "even things out."

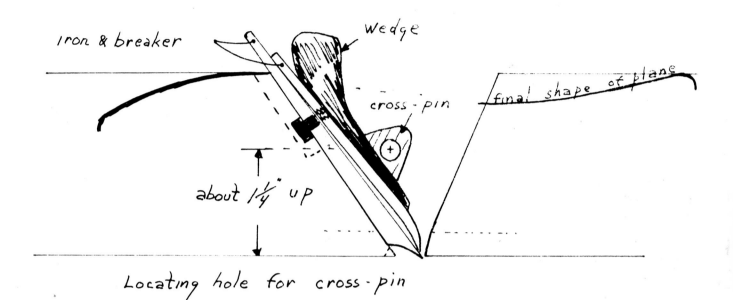

Locating hole for cross-pin

Have everything neat, and prepare carefully for gluing. When you do glue, remember to place the cross-pin into one of the side pieces and leave it there while you brush on glue. (One can forget such an obvious detail.) Use a strip of wood clamped along the bottom to align its two halves; remove this before the glue dries. Glue neatly; wipe the opening clean inside. Give the glue time to dry. If you have made the plane so that it does not need an added shoe, you are now near your goal. Very, very carefully, take a few cuts with another plane, or on the jointer, and bring the opening up to where the iron just barely begins to come through. Watch out! The opening grows quickly; it is so easy to spoil the plane, or at least cause a lot of extra work on it. One of the most common accidents in making a plane is an opening suddenly become too large.

If you need a hardwood shoe, very hard, close-grained wood, not too brittle, is best—though very hard wood is apt to *be* brittle. Choose a piece so that its "fur" is back along the bottom; it's less apt to chip out around the opening. The shoe can be in one piece, and I like it that way, but the chances of making the opening too large, or chipping it when cutting through, are very real. A way of avoiding this is to fit a small wood insert at the front of the opening: it is easier to do, its front corners can be nicely rounded, and later, when the plane wears down, this insert is handily replaced. Likewise, a new plane that is not quite perfect can be saved by cutting into the one-piece shoe, or the body of a "whole" plane, and making this insert exactly the way you want it.

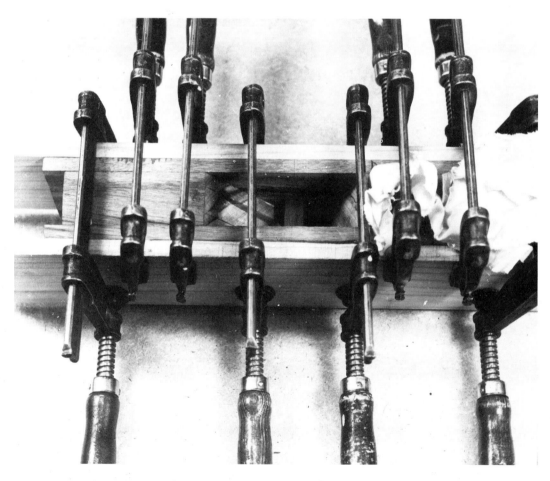

Gluing: cross-pin is in place.

Single-piece shoe: laying out for cutting through. Care must be taken not to chip or crack edges of final opening.

Separate insert for flat-bottom plane. Final thin opening is "simpler" and more apt to be exactly as desired.

Sooner or later, if you like wooden planes, you will be making them with rounded bottoms—these planes open new possibilities of shapes and surfaces. It is a definite advantage to use an insert here, fitting it patiently to the exact curve of the iron. Do this by stages, first the width, then round the front corners, mark the extremities of the curve—and finally carve and file the insert, making a neat transition from the flat forward slope of the original sawn opening to the curve you need. Glue the insert by wedging it tightly forward and let the glue settle for a day or so. Then work the plane bottom to a perfect finish. If you make a one-piece shoe for a flat plane, mark it carefully for the opening and cut slowly down, with the piece clamped tight and a layer of plywood or Masonite between to protect your workbench. Check it as you cut, align the sloping surface of the planing angle exactly, keep cutting slowly until the iron—in position—comes almost but not quite through. Locate the shoe with two thin dowels—or even brads—at the far ends, which you will saw off when you shape the plane. Recheck the fit, then glue the shoe on as neatly as you did the other parts. The care and attention you devote to each step will pay off.

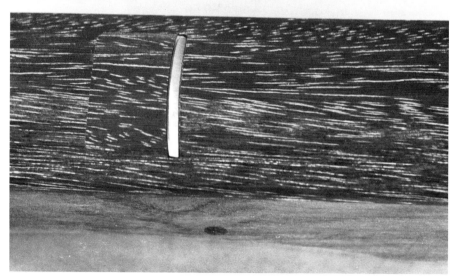

Insert, carefully fitted to shape of plane-iron along cutting edge, is the best way of obtaining a fine opening on all curved-bottom planes.

Now you work the plane down to that tiny opening for the sharp iron and those light, smooth cuts. But before the results begin to come, you have to think about finishing the edge of the breaker, polishing it, sharpening the iron, making a wedge that is pleasantly shaped; one with a low angle, a hollow for the protruding end of the screw—and a thick end suitable for tapping with a small hammer. Lots of details, each important!

You have put your plane together; leaving it simply as a block of wood. Now try using it just to get the feel. Think of the way you'd like to shape it in order to work comfortably in various ways. I shape my planes as little as possible; my earlier ones were more bumpy—and more confused. These bumps and humps do fit the hands, but they tend to keep the hands there even when the work calls for another hold. We use our planes in different ways for dif-

ferent kinds of work, for surfaces, edges, curves—we enjoy ourselves most, and work best, when all this feels right. So try to discover these variations for yourself and gradually, step by step, develop an ideal shape for each plane as you use it.

Unless made unduly intricate, the entire shape of the finished plane can be done on a bandsaw. The resulting surfaces and edges are only touched up with a file or knife. The sawn wood is pleasant in the hand when working, and does not tend to slip.

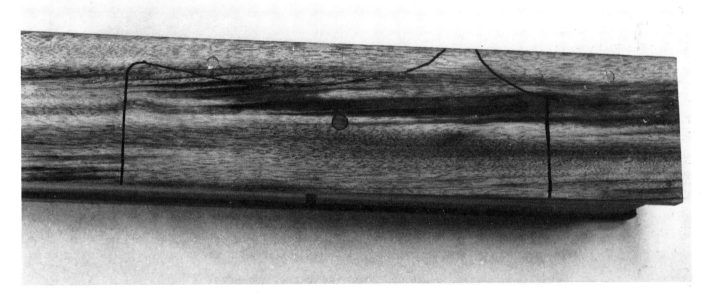

Polishing planes, about five to seven
inches long.

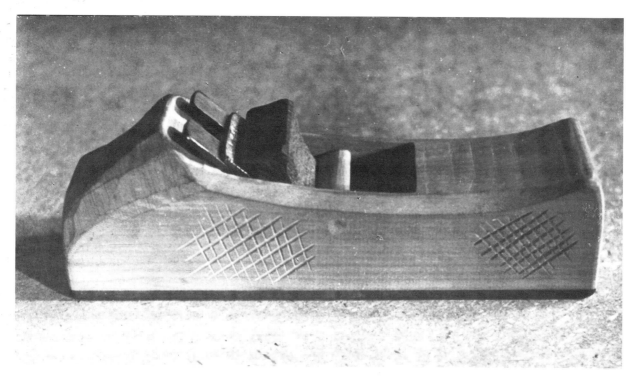

Now and then students put fancy handles on their planes, especially on the larger ones. To me this goes against the very purpose of these planes—that of having them low on the work and easy in one's hands. By easy I mean being able to change our grip as we work. At most one can glue a shoulder, or thumbrest, just behind the iron, and then shape this into the back of the plane. Jointer planes can have "nostrils"—recesses cut into the sides of the nose where your fingers seem to rest naturally. But regular handles back there, or knobs up front—no. I'll admit they can be decorative. Granted, too, some of us may feel lost without them at first—we all started woodworking using (iron) planes with handles.

Still, I believe you will find these simple low planes easier to work with if you give them the chance. Also I suspect that some planes seem to call for handles because they were made clumsier than they should be.

Here, at the risk of being a bore, I will list some of the most common errors that occur when one makes planes like this. The first, obviously, is that in planning the position of the iron with its opening we make simple little mistakes and the opening, too large, is there grinning at us. Another is when we drill the hole for the cross-pin too high up, and this spoils the final shape of our tool. Or when we crowd the pin against the iron, and can't get a wedge in there. Error number four: we do not pay enough attention to the shape and polished edge of the breaker. These are basic points; pay close attention to them, please!

When first trying out the plane, remember: it should cut well from the start and beautifully before long: as soon as you have a fine flat bottom, a small opening, sharp iron and well-made breaker you have everything needed to produce a perfect cut. That flat bottom must really be flat and be kept flat, if the plane is to behave properly. When you first make the plane, true the bottom by working it—with the iron backed up a bit—against a piece of belt sandpaper on a jointer or saw table. Later—

Truing plane bottom. Piece of belt sandpaper on jointer or other flat surface. Plane iron backed up clear of abrasive—but wedged to normal tension, as when plane is in use.

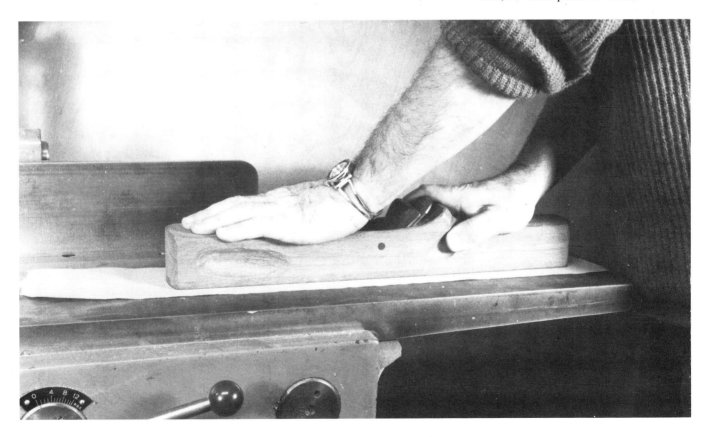

perhaps after a month or so—you may discover that the plane is behaving strangely; especially if it is a jointer plane, it may show a tendency to bow. You can't see this, but it is noticeable in the work. The strain of the wedge is causing a bow, and you need to true the plane. Another crankiness is caused by very hard wear on the bottom just in front of the iron itself: you can check that the shoe is not hollowed here by laying a straightedge across it.

If the plane scrapes as you work, the breaker-edge may not be right: rough or at the wrong angle where it meets the iron. The slope of the plane where the iron rests may not be clean and true; perhaps you left a spot of glue there. An iron that is not sharp enough will put that final paper-thin shaving just out of reach.

I presume all these things are meaningful to you, and you pay attention to each detail, since you want a result that justifies the effort. And it is an effort, really, getting to that beautiful cut, a soft whispering sound and a shaving coming up in a curl or almost straight, shimmering in the light.

If the shaving is being creased and folded, there is something wrong with the breaker, or at the opening itself. The shavings should swish up by themselves.

Adjust the breaker: a margin of about 1/32 inch for fine work and just under 1/16 inch for general use is a good way to begin.

In addition to all these points, you must have care and patience to make the final small adjustments which are the difference between just a tool—and something better. The more you expect from your plane, the more important each detail becomes.

Take the matter of tapping the iron and wedge into final position for the cut you want to make on a very special wood. We are often told to sight along the bottom from in front, give the other end a whack or two—"and when you see the edge of the iron you are ready to go." Maybe! But a good shaving is paper-thin, certainly less than a 1/64 inch. The *slightest* change of the iron—if it is a hair too far out, or leans a degree to one side—makes a crucial difference. We simply must be patient. And sensitive: one does not tune a Stradivarius with a monkey wrench.

So slide the iron and breaker into what you judge will be their final position; you can sight against the opening. As you do this, slip the wedge in, too, supporting it from below (you have the plane bottom-side up). Sight along the plane from *behind*, and with a small hammer tap, tap lightly until you see that first

thin glint. Tighten the wedge a bit. Swing the plane to and fro with the light playing on the cutting edge, and get it absolutely even. But keep it a thin glinting line. Try a cut; then, if need be, make a final tap or two. In time all this will be habit; you will be able to adjust your plane as quickly as any metal one with its screws and levers. You will do this with a finer degree of sensitivity and with better results, which is very satisfying—like being able to tune a delicate musical instrument perfectly before playing it well. But you do need a good ear. Using these planes has long since become natural for me; I'm apt to forget it was not always so.

Now, you say, I've made the thing; how do I get it to work right? You've tinkered with it a bit and discovered how sensitive (or fickle) it can be, and even shaped it more or less as you want and now, starting to use it you bump into trouble. Bump is the word; at the start and the finish of each stroke the going is bumpy. There is a jerk-and-jump as we begin the cut and then at the far end we get another jolt as the nose of the plane goes off the deep end. At both ends the piece is uneven, we are not making a smooth cut. And to work this way doesn't feel right. What's with our plane anyhow?

First positioning of iron. Wedge only
pressed in. Tap plane to bring iron just
under surface of plane bottom. Then
carefully tap back of iron to final
position. Sight from *behind,* against
light, and adjust iron exactly parallel
to shoe. Tap wedge home and see that
iron has not changed position.

The fact that you sense the faults is a good sign. Calm down, and make one complete stroke in slow motion. At the start you press the *nose* of the plane down, while with the other hand you push more than you press. Actually, you hardly press at all back there; your elbow is down low. One way to practice is to remove your hand from behind the plane and with the other press-and-pull into the cut. This is not the way you will be doing it later, but it proves a point: the *front* of the plane is all-important at the beginning of each stroke. And because a gradually widening cut starts easier than a sudden wide one, you should form the habit of starting your cuts on the diagonal. Let the plane slant almost forty-five degrees at first and gradually straighten it out.

Along the middle area of each cut, press evenly with both hands; a signal is that your hand and elbow behind the plane want to come up a little. Your hands and arms are relaxed because the force and pressure are so natural as you lean forward. It's a sort of coasting.

You finish your practice cut by lifting your hand from the nose of the plane and just push-pressing at the *back* with the other until the iron has stopped whispering and left the wood—without the plane having first tipped forward and jerked.

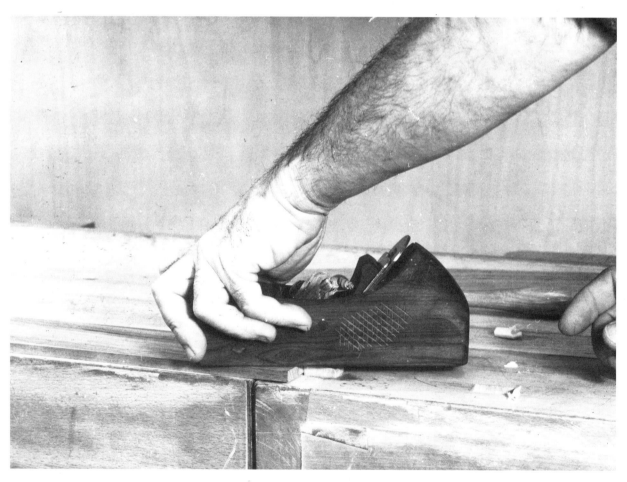

Three principal stages of a natural and effective stroke with a wood plane.

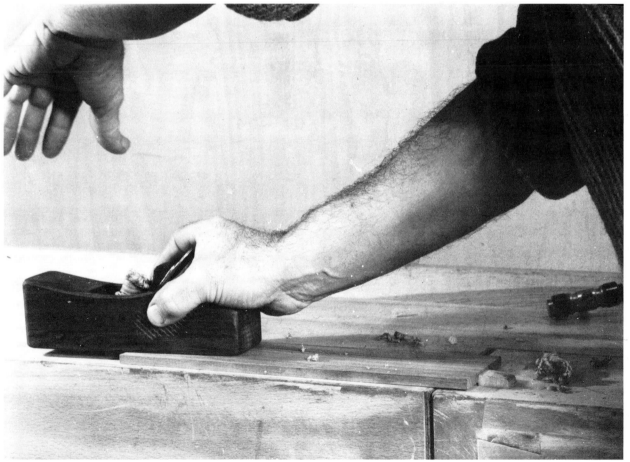

So there are three stages: start, glide, finish. Press at front, press-and-push, press at back—one smooth motion and an even cut. If this is not what you experience, you are probably using too much arm and not enough body. With only the arms working, your motions are jerky and hesitant. But the final result you will arrive at will be an easy rocking movement—hands, arms, torso, legs, all the way from the plane and through your body and down to the floor. A rocking forward and back, all in one as you start, coast, finish and return. Unhurried, *firm*—and so easy. Like a perfect forehand stroke in tennis. No jerking, no violence: trying to overpower the work is only a sign of ignorance. Plane properly and you will get a lot of work done without tiring: you can work for hours this way, and feel good.

Don't shift your feet unless you have to. With a natural stance you can plane pieces three feet long or even more in one satisfying stroke.

Planing edges for jointing is more difficult than smoothing surfaces for most of us. The tendency is to twist a bit as we move forward with the plane—it's just something we tend to do, the way we are put together, and move. On a short stroke it isn't apparent, but with longer pieces the twist or wind in our planing becomes a bother. Don't try to keep things right by holding the plane very tensely, and steering. No use! Relax instead. Practice a very even stroke, notice the result—and if there is a

twist (usually to the right at the far end), correct this by changing the *balance* of the plane in your hands. Try letting the nose swing to the left a little at the far side of the cut. Let the weight of the plane in relation to the narrow piece help you: planing like this is a sort of balancing act or dance. It's all balance and rhythm.

One final hint. I have found that by keeping the top of my planes flat across—that is, at right angles to the sides even though curved lengthwise—I can better relate to the cut I am making in jointing; the top surface of my plane is "as I'm cutting," or close to it. This is only one way of getting your bearings. But it is handy especially when you are planing bevels, such as for coopered doors.

Another basic use of these planes—at least of the shorter ones—is a circular motion while you work a surface flat where the grain is rowed or otherwise difficult to cut in one direction only. You press down hard on the plane with both hands *atop* it, and more with your arms and shoulders now than before. You do this circular motion while moving along the surface. It's the most neutral way to cut, and you can use it on difficult grain, or where two surfaces come together, as in a frame or other flat joint.

The planes I am describing are low, simple shapes for the hands. For *a* hand as well: holding a smallish plane in one hand while you round an edge or work a small piece of wood to thickness gives a miniature pleasure

which is very intense because it is so close; both effort and results are right there in your hands.

After it becomes natural and right for you, the experience of planing is an inner dimension: a condition rather than an activity. A state of serene satisfaction. Your attention is on what is happening, on the changes taking place in the wood rather than on your hands or the plane or the fact of an effort you are making. You watch the results of your movements instead of thinking about them. Like when you've hit the ball well, and know it—without remembering the stroke. You will see a surface change from dull to clear: rough-sawn or even machined it is dull and as you plane it clears in little waves, the burnished patches are spreading like sunshine touching a field under scattered clouds.

Another time you watch an edge as you round it, see its shadow lines behind each stroke, stop to run a finger along it, cock your head to catch the light a little better as you relate this edge to a proportion, a shading, a part of something no drawing and no machine can convey.

There is a generally accepted, oversimplified concept of wooden planes that ignores the sensitivity with which the downward curve of the breaker should be formed and polished, the hardly perceptible adjustments that make the difference between a perfect cut and just a cut. There are tell-tale signs of a plane being out of tune: knowing how it should be retuned and what movements harmonize with the various uses of this high-spirited tool are important.

To a beginner, this search—going from a mere generality through many small discoveries to an understanding of what a fine plane can do for you—can be very frustrating. At times one wishes to throw the whole thing on the floor, every cranky bit. Also there is an even greater danger; you can get exasperated and simply quit.

I think it is important that the first plane or two you make bring fair results, because otherwise you will be disappointed—and may not care to try again. The balance between success and something less is often delicate. We need to pass a certain point, cross a threshold of discovery where we say, "Oh, *that's* what it is about. Now I'm beginning to see. . . ."

Otherwise we presume, as most people do, that a plane is a plane is a plane, and leave it. This is a pity, since for a certain kind of craftsman a plane can be more than a tool. It can be a beautiful instrument, a joy to use. It can bring results that truly do show in the work, the piece itself. A fine plane is a time-saver and a labor-saver; it more than repays the care and love you give it. It is at its best a part of you, your hands and eye and your innermost hopes as you work.

I hope your first exercise in making a plane will encourage further experiment and even better results—until the whole thing will open up and you will perceive the true possibilities of this fine tool, this instrument, the cabinetmaker's Stradivarius.

Keep at it, and make planes to fit your aims, various kinds for your work as it develops through the years. Try different lengths, weights, shapes. Rounded planes, double curved ones, large and small—whatever you may need. It does not take too much effort to make a fine plane, once you have got the knack of it.

If you feel that wood is a rich and wonderful material to work with, and want to come closer to your wood, to be on more intimate terms with it—then a real plane is the shortest distance to that final result and final enjoyment.

Using a small (six-inch) plane.

Planes with bottoms shaped to various
curves.

Tool cabinet near main workbench.

SPOKESHAVES, ETC.

By now it is evident that I do a great deal of work with my various planes. Besides the flat ones, I have made a number that are rounded: also a few whose bottom is a compound curve—with these I can work a gentle hollow. I altered one or two of my old flat polishing planes by sawing the bottom on a slight arc that enables me to shape inside arcs such as on table legs and stretchers. All these planes, when I use them properly, help me to obtain the final shape and surface I want without having to rough-sand and then polish. If I must use sandpaper, it will be only fine grit: I'll use it as little as possible, very lightly.

We all do pieces where the end-grain shows; in fact it is a part of the decorative side of our work. *The pattern of end grain often tells something special about that particular wood.* If we rasp and sand end grain, we fill the pores, change the tone of the wood, and deprive the grain pattern of the clarity which is such an important part of its appeal. For reasons explained later, some of my cabinets are doweled together. This gives me the freedom to shape the sides of a piece as I will, or angle them a little—and then follow that shape with roundings or bevels, for instance, that give shadings and character to the top and bottom pieces.

Sometimes, because of the nature of a particular wood, I have to plane, file, and then finely sand these edges. But more often I work them all the way with a polishing plane and spokeshave where the grain permits—and with a small, low-angle Stanley block plane along the end grain itself.

Credit where credit is due: the #60 1/2 plane is a very nice tool. Its edges need attention, since they are sharp and unpleasant to begin with, and the back of the adjustment front piece should be filed neatly parallel to the cutting edge of an iron that is straight and true: some of us may want to remove the lever under the knob up there. With this done, and *the front piece moved back until the opening is paper-thin, one can cut cleanly on all sorts of end-grain shapes,* those outside radii which are often difficult to get really smooth. The difficulty of polishing such shapes with a block plane (or any plane for that matter) arises from the opening in the plane being too large: a bit of the curve as we work "sinks into" the opening, causing the iron to bite and tear. Thus, if you set your plane finely for a straight cut or a lesser curve, and then with the same set try to work a tighter curve— you get a bad result, no matter how sharp the iron. But with the block plane properly trimmed and set very fine, you can hold it snugly in one hand and round even the most delicate curves and corners to the shape you want and a pleasing, clean-cut luster. When you can, hold the plane on a diagonal as you work.

During one of my stays at the

Iron block-plane (Stanley #60½).

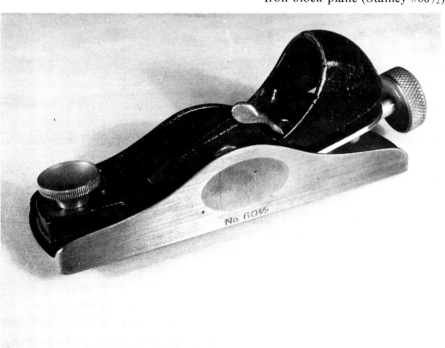

The opening of such a plane should be
set as thin as possible for the work to
be done.

A more usual and less efficient
opening.

Rochester Institute of Technology in Rochester, New York, there was a student who did furniture of the sculptured sort, mostly stacked. He used a lot of wood and did all kinds of weird shapes with lovely little planes he had made for this purpose. The planes themselves were no more than three inches long, of rosewood, with brass fittings and a pivoted brass yoke—perhaps ten inches long—that ended in a handle. He had them in several shapes, and with the handle he got a lot of power into each stroke—usually on the pull. He used these tools with great skill, cutting away steadily at even the hardest wood. The resulting forms were interesting, though rough, since the planes had no breaker, the surfaces needed to be worked with a scraper and then sanded.

There are reasons for comparing spokeshaves with planes. Both are classic cabinetmaker's tools. Both can be made by the craftsman who will later use them. And again, as with planes, there is a great difference between just a spokeshave—and a spokeshave that is finely tuned. I don't say "a fine spokeshave," because one of the several spokeshaves available to us can be made to produce a really fine result—without being what I would call a fine tool. I am speaking now of the Kuntz spokeshave with the adjustable front edge, or jaw. This is a standard tool, not expensive and not very well made by some measures: the pivot pins are unsteady, the casting leaves something to be desired, the blade could be of better steel and properly finished. But—and it is an important but—by tuning it up and handling it with care you can get beautiful results with this tool. The pivoting part needs to be gone over carefully: rounded at its front, trued along the opening: the entire contact surface should be softened all round with a file so it will not dig, or leave scratches, the blade needs to be polished on the up side and then made truly sharp. After which you can test your spokeshave: if every detail is cared for and the opening set for the particular curve you are working—the cuts will be very, very fine, and the resulting edges or curves a pleasure to touch. On wood like English brown oak, elm, or cherry, it would indeed be a loss to then sand away such results. Though some do just that.

As I see it, the Kuntz spokeshave is neither particularly well made nor sturdy—it won't stand up to the really heavy work for which a Stanley spokeshave with its single-piece body and two set screws is better. (Even the latter needs some attention around the contact surface and the opening before one can use it with any degree of pleasure; after that it is reliable.)

Spokeshaves: some common types.

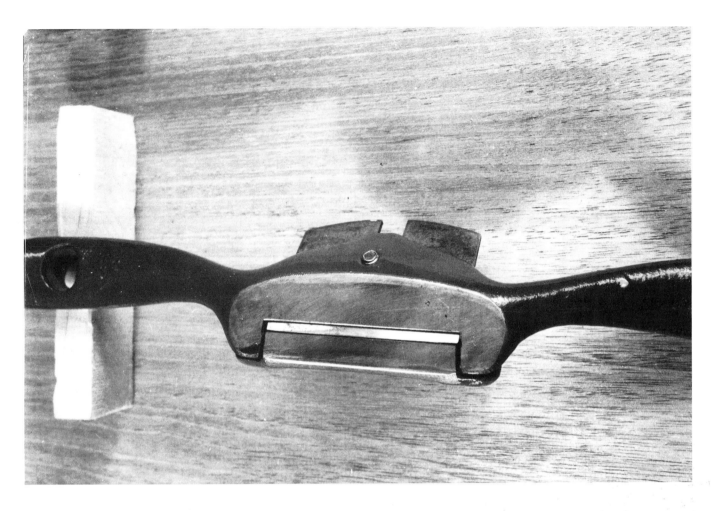

The Kuntz spokeshave with adjustable
(pivot) front.

The traditional spokeshaves were of wood. Their history is long and their uses many, which may be a reason why at least one is still being manufactured today: surely it is not because wood ones cut better or last longer than the metal ones. The straight and simple English Marples used to be boxwood with a brass inlay at the front. Now, I believe, it is made in beech, without the inlay, which means the wood surface around the cutting area will wear very quickly. Fitting a metal edge here helps. But there is another reason why I hesitate to recommend this tool for all-purpose work: the fairly narrow body gives a small radius of contact, and makes the tool a bit tricky to handle. Either it tends to dig and chatter—or it won't cut at all. The blade with its two prongs let into the body is not always easy to adjust finely enough; even when set, it tends to shift. Nor can it be sharpened without special care, since it has a downward bevel which has to be reached between the two bent prongs. Still: with a metal inlay to save wear, this spokeshave has one advantage—it is suitable for working rather tight curves with small inside radii where the other standard spokeshaves are unable to reach.

There are several other types of spokeshaves, large and small, iron and even brass, flat or for inside curves—and even half-round. The pros and cons of these are a matter of personal usage and opinion.

Some years ago there used to be small, very fine drawknives: I remember using these for days on end while making sailboat masts of beautiful straight-grained Sitka spruce. Such a tool is handy for rough shaping; even the larger models we get nowadays will do for this work.

When it comes to scrapers, there is a good deal I do not

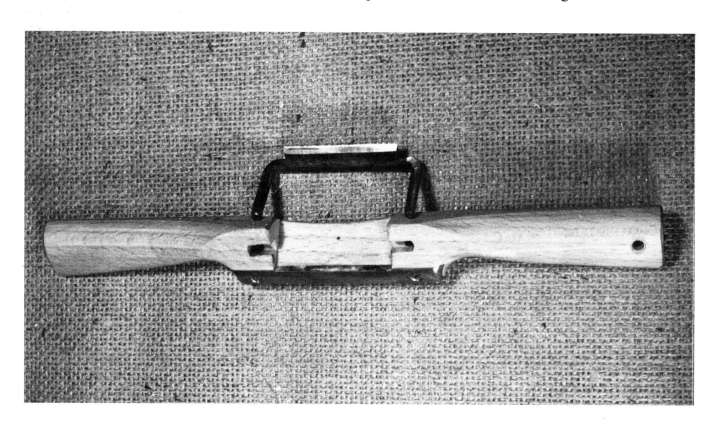

Marples wood spokeshave. The metal (brass) edge was added later by the user.

106

know; many of their finer points have eluded me because my use of scrapers has been limited. A person making musical instruments would have a variety of scrapers, some of them special, including the thin, highly polished ones used for finishing work such as on lacquered surfaces. On occasions I have made coopered doors and such curved things of Andaman padouk or other rowed wood; these I planed to a rough shape and then worked with scrapers which I had refiled to the shapes I wanted. Some of these scrapers were originally the standard straight kind. Most proved to be usable, though the quality varied with the manufacturer. So did the thickness.

There are finely finished scrapers of hardened steel, intended for treated surfaces, and the more common sort, also of steel, but fairly soft and often with the sides scratched by production machines. At one time I obtained some pieces of old bandsaw blade of the type used by sawmills; these I had cut to size—they made excellent scrapers, some of which I shaped for special small roundings and inside corners. I even put a wooden handle on the narrow ones.

There is a lot of discussion as to how scrapers should be filed, polished, burnished, and laid (or curled). Most of this is in books. Some advocate doing the curl in one firm stroke of the burnisher, others (including myself) prefer a series of light back-and-forth strokes at a gradually increasing angle. All of us first file the edge and then hone it—a few hone both the edge and the surfaces. Whichever you do, *use a separate stone for this:* even when you swing the scraper to and fro as you hone, it will leave the stone uneven after a time. Use a fine flat file, hone carefully—even small marks on the scraper edge will result in scratches like those of coarse sandpaper, as deep or even deeper, since we press as we work. It's exasperating to have done a surface with a scraper you think is all right (since it does cut) and sand very fine and apply a finish—only to hold the result up to the light and discover those scratches.

Though a scraper for flat surfaces should have a straight edge, its corner can well be made to rise a trifle so as to avoid accidents; we are apt to work wood that is uneven, or to press down on one end of our scraper.

Bear in mind: *despite its name, a scraper should cut, and not just scrape.* You want fine, even shavings—not mere crumbs and dust. Also take into account that most soft woods and some not so soft (elm, mahogany, larch) are not really intended to be worked to a smooth finish with scrapers.

As a scraper gets dull it only scrapes. It can be relaid once or twice before you have to file and whet it again. But work cautiously: it is very easy to crumple or dent the fine edges when doing this rescue work.

If there is a conclusion to be drawn from these few observations about cutting tools, it is this: I believe a large part of the enjoyment and the satisfaction of our craft—and by satisfaction I mean not only the doing but also the result—lies in discovering the finer points of each of these tools. We will not tire, or go stale, so long as we are aware of sensitivities yet to be achieved, information that we can turn into our own personal experiences—experiences that enable us to make not only pretty shavings, but also a sort of music.

Our experience often begins at school; our start comes at a time when we are relatively free—we are not yet involved in setting up a shop, but can think about doing so. We aren't as yet under pressure, we don't need to weigh each hour or day against rent, materials, or—for better or for worse—income. So this is a good time in our lives. We can experiment with tools, make some and find others which we hope to buy, and then keep looking. Doing this without too much worry adds to the pleasure. It is a pleasure we should allow ourselves if possible later on in life as well—even though we have to pay a higher price for it then.

Oak cabinet. The detail shows spoke-shave-shaped edges and parts of stand (legs, stretchers).

108

SHARPENING TOOLS

Just as sharpness can mean different things to different woodworkers, so too the ways in which we go about getting tools sharp are different.

I recall a scene at a certain school: the beginning of the term, fellows checking out tools and sharpening them. Someone at the electric grinder is grinding chisels. The machine whines, spitting sparks, smoke rises, and a nasty shade of blue is creeping up the piece of steel in the boy's tense hands. He looks pleadingly at the instructor who is just passing through the shop. This pillar of knowledge says, "Oh, it takes years to learn to sharpen tools properly," and walks on.

So much is wrong about that situation!

Disappointments are not always a necessary part of learning—if deep enough, they can set us back too far. They keep us from reaching just that positive stage of learning which is the threshold to further knowledge because it encourages experiment and enjoyable results.

Using an electric grinder without mishap is difficult. The heat generated, the often inadequate toolrests, the way one feels uptight about it all—these do not make for a pleasant experience. Then, too, because the machine is not likable, you are apt to be in a hurry using it.

There are other ways of sharpening tools. Take away the "electric" part, and you remove a lot of the trouble. "Ah!" someone says, "a primitivist: he wants us to use the old sandstone wheel." Not quite. The sandstone wheel, although pleasant and romantic, is in my opinion not ideal for small tools. One reason is that the large diameter produces very little hollow grind. And hollow-grinding is desirable, as I will try to explain.

During two visits to American schools I had with me a small hand-type grinder, a clamp-on model such as I use in my own workshop. We set this up as shown in the photos here, and used it continuously. It was a discovery. After a few practice tries the students were able to use it well—and enjoyed doing so.

Hand-type tool grinder with toolrest of wood as described in text.

Plane-irons and chisels were transformed: scratched factory surfaces and rough edges disappeared, tools became sharp and smooth—and were kept that way, because a bit of regrinding now and then was easy, too. There was no longer good reason for postponing sharpening tools. We used the electric grinder for rough work, but only for that.

The setup is very simple—with one exception: a hand-type bench grinder of good quality suitable for a five- or six-inch wheel may not always be easy to find in this age of tinny convenience and electrical do-it-quick. Still, these hand grinders are available at some of the better suppliers.

The one-by-five or one-by-six inch carborundum wheel should be of a fairly fine grit: we do not want later on to whet away the hollow while trying to get past the scratches and obtain a sharp edge.

Probably there is a metal toolrest of sorts on the grinder. These toolrests—despite the advertisements—are not ideal. I do believe the person who makes a proper toolrest of wood, as shown, will discover its advantages soon enough.

Make this rest out of fairly thick (three- or four-inch) medium-hard wood such as maple or ash. In a block about four inches high and six inches long, band-saw an opening suitable for the clamp that will hold the rest in place when you use it. Bevel the upper edge of this block, and add the top part, protruding some three or

four inches at a total height and angle close to the one you will be using most when grinding your plane-irons. Set up the grinder and check this as you make the toolrest. As to final adjustment for various tools: with the help of a thin wooden wedge you can obtain the exact angle you want each time. A mark or two on the wedge will help. A lengthwise groove about 1/2 inch deep saves wear and tear on fingertips and makes for easier holding.

For grinding chisels, etc., you can have a separate toolrest with a narrow top surface (1 or 1 1/2 inches wide) that allows the flared shank and also the handle of the chisel to hang free, yet lending support to the short flat part of the tool nearest the cutting edge. Keep in mind that the angle for chisels will be different from that on plane-irons; make the block accordingly.

Sharpening tools this way is easier than an outside description can convey. It is all a matter of rhythm—of relaxing and developing an easy motion. You wind with one hand and hold with the other, both hands moving all the while. The rotation of the wheel is towards the tool

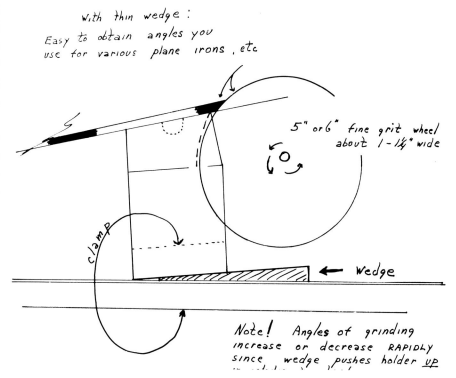

With thin wedge: Easy to obtain angles you use for various plane irons, etc

5" or 6" fine grit wheel about 1 - 1½" wide

← Wedge

clamp

Note! Angles of grinding increase or decrease RAPIDLY since wedge pushes holder UP

Grinding chisel with help of narrower
toolrest of wood.

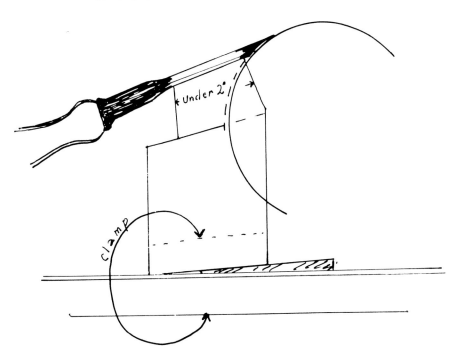

*Tool-rest with narrow top
provides riding surface for
flat underside of chisel,
allowing shank & handle
to be free . . . .*

Under 2°

Clamp

being ground. Work with ease, not too fast nor very slow—with a medium spin and a steady to-and-fro of the hand holding the tool. There is a natural tendency to hesitate at the far end of each stretch with the iron: you will find the edge beginning to be rounded at the corners—which is wrong. Practice counteracting this by a slight speeding up there; this results in a comparative "hesitating" at the middle of each swing. Develop this technique, but do not stop with the tool against the spinning wheel or force the work. In time you will be able to sense exactly whether or not the edge is as you want it. Even the learning is enjoyable: no real risks involved, no burning, no deep dips along the edge of the tool.

Not only do we sharpen tools easily this way, but also the occasional regrinding that is a part of keeping them perfect is no problem. We do not avoid the process, and postpone grinding while we continue to use cutting tools that are not as sharp as they should be.

Honing is just as important as grinding. Perhaps even more so, since we need to hone more often, and it is, at least in practice, the final test of sharpening tools.

You can hone in a way that preserves the advantages of a hollow-ground edge—or you can hone improperly, and lose that advantage. By honing improperly I mean one of two things: using the wrong stone or the wrong technique. At worst, we do both.

A properly ground edge need not be honed on a rough stone. If you have used a fine-grit wheel, you can usually go directly to an India or a soft Arkansas surface. How you use this stone—and later the hard Arkansas—is as vital as the quality of the stone itself. All too often we are taught to use a back-and-forth stroke along the length of the stone. Usually this stroke is too long: because of this and the way our arm is put together we get a rocking motion; the iron describes an arc which in turn results in a tendency to first flatten and then "round over" the sloping edge—wiping out the hollow. If you continue with this method, you will get a dip in the opposite direction—a sort of bluntness. *Keep that hollow-ground slope for as long as possible.* It gives a proper rest when you are honing. It tells us how much we have honed, and how well. It is another kind of guide too: as long as we have a bit of it visible we can simply rehone—several times during a period of concentrated work—instead of having to rush off to the grinder.

When you hone, long strokes are less easy to control than short ones. To-and-fro is not as suitable as round and round or, even better, a short sidewise pivoting. Use various areas of the stone to keep the wear even, but the area used during any one stroke is small.

Whetting. India or Washita oilstone can be used directly after grinding with fine-grit wheel.

Honing to final edge on hard Arkansas stone. Use light, short, steady movement.

As to the much-discussed bow, or slight curve advocated by some: keep it very, very slight indeed. Hardly perceptible. An ordinary nicely cut shaving is paper-thin, your iron is 1 1/2 or 1 3/4 inches wide. *If the iron curves more than a hair, each cut will be unnecessarily narrow. Observe this fact.* Don't whet too long: those whiskers along the cutting edge won't disappear unless you use a light touch and the right strokes. How you hold that iron (or chisel) is of great importance. One tendency is to hold it too high up, and not to support it properly. We suppose that the ground bevel is support enough. Well, by itself it is not. This fact increases the probability of rocking, the iron tipping and tilting on its narrow sloping edge. Try holding the piece way down as low as possible, the fingertips of your fore- and index fingers nearly touching the stone. Support the iron a bit higher up with your thumb, ring and (or) little finger. Lightly! You will feel how the tool "settles" into position on the stone, and then you need only to keep it that way while you hone. Using short, light strokes you will sense how the iron stays in position, and after a while this condition will be the only natural one as you work.

Plane-iron ready for use. Later it can be rehoned four or five times before grinding is necessary.

Plane-iron ground but not honed: notice slight hollow, and also burred edge. This burr is easily removed without losing hollow-grind.

The "other," or flat, side of an iron or chisel is as much in need of attention as the side you have ground. Nowadays tools are seldom what they should be. Even so-called fine ones come to us with this surface uneven and full of scratches under that nice sprayed-on lacquer. *No well-ground and honed edge will ever be really sharp, much less stay sharp, unless both its sides are polished and smooth.* This often means tedious work at first, yes, but when the "other" side is perfect, the tool needs only half as much attention later on.

Most of the stones we use for honing are called oilstones, and maybe as a result of this we tend to use oil on them. I mean machine oil, sewing-machine oil, and the like. These oils clog the stone. This must be experienced to be proved—one way to prove it is to try a really thin liquid such as cutting oil. It is better, though I myself have not found anything to surpass plain old kerosene. Good, and cheap. Even when carefully used, an oilstone will in time become somewhat uneven. You can prolong the life of your best ones by using them only for tools with a fairly wide edge, such as plane irons, knives, and larger chisels. Keep a separate stone or two for narrow items, small chisels, scrapers, and the like, which tend to groove the surface.

Whetting upper, or flat, side of chisel or plane-iron is as important as is the ground edge. Remove all scratches from the cutting end of the new tool: after this, only a minimum of honing is necessary at each sharpening.

A stone can be trued by sprinkling a suitable grinding compound (powder) on a piece of glass and rubbing the stone (wet) against this. Or you can go to a potter, and ask him to true it for you as he does the bottoms of his pots.

Sharpening tools is less difficult than some people suppose. Keeping tools sharp is even easier. If you have several irons for each of your planes, and a few extra chisels in the most-used sizes, you can rotate these in a way that will not interrupt the flow of other work. This habit is very important, since to do good work year after year you need sharp tools, the sense of being at ease, and the feeling that all is going well.

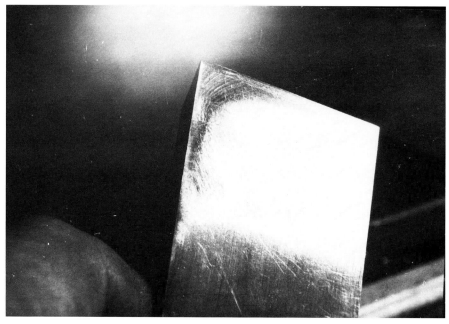

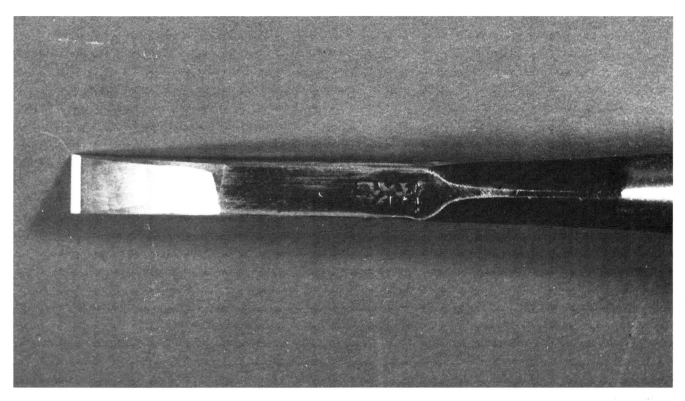

Tools sharpened on hand-type grinder
and then honed to fine edge.

SANDING

To insist on using cutting tools only—all the way—is to be bullheaded and ignorant. "Different woods, different methods" is not so much a rule as a reflection of our sensitivity towards our particular material. We make something out of ash, or elm, or maybe pearwood, and because the wood cuts well, giving us clear surfaces and nice burnished edges—or perhaps a silvery sheen—we work almost everything with our planes, spokeshave, chisels, knives. We are drawn towards a condition of feeling that leads to methods. There is a relationship between what we feel as we use our tools—and the character of the piece. Cutting wood cleanly, we become aware of shimmer, luster, simple lines and surfaces in uncluttered objects.

When we use fine cutting tools in the right way, there is a closeness—better yet, a directness—about our work; the intention, method, and result are all there honestly balanced. So for some of us wood usually wants to be nicely cut. Not ground into crumbs or dust, but cut. Cleanly, leaving traces of the methods used. So, naturally, we feel an aversion toward files and sandpaper and some other things which can pass unnamed. Which is not to say that we never use sandpaper or files: we do use them. But as seldom and as lightly as possible. They are connected with a few special woods, rowed and stubborn like padouk or bubinga. And with shapes that are a compromise to the difficult qualities of some nonetheless decorative woods which we use with a mixture of reluctance and fascination.

If you have a tendency towards engineered sharpness or to organic flowing things, showiness of one kind or another, then your whole approach to wood is different. You are apt to abandon cutting tools along the way and grind, rasp, rough-sand, polish by all sorts of efficient methods. Or maybe you bend wood into fanciful shapes that do not easily lend themselves to cutting tools. It is all a matter of a personal relationship to your work.

A certain kind of person can design objects to be made of wood, and make them—and still they won't be wood. Not really. They reach us not as wood, but as shapes and colors that happen to be wood, but could just as well be another material. Some of this work is sharp and stiff and studied in its forms—sanded and then lacquered, with maybe a bit of plastic here and there. The result is decorative, but one wants to ask, why wood?

A popular idiom nowadays is that of slick shapes and tapered edges. Still another sought-after result is a kind of heavy-handed, *bloated* furniture. Really a take-off on good, functional predecessors: but clumsy, overdimensioned. It may get by as being "whimsical," but it is unskilled work.

I can't help but feel, sometimes, that much of this is a result of trying to be extraordinary in a rather ordinary and competitive way. Many of the ideas are good. Some of the craftsmen are good. But somewhere something has gone wrong, and efficiency is taking over. Or maybe competition within the same sort of originality. More and more shapes are being done with pneumatic tools, electric routers; surfaces are belt sanded, edges rasped and then sanded once, twice. I don't think it is always because of a lack of skill. What, then? Most craftsmen have a legitimate excuse: they have to make a living. They haven't made it big, they are struggling and can't always do pieces as they would like to—at least not yet.

All right. That is an understandable excuse. We are most of us fighting to survive, honestly hoping to reach a point where we will be able to do what we want the way we want to do it—and receive due compensation for it. But there are those who are getting a good price for their work, and have a reputation. They should have freedom. The pieces they make are already expensive: would fine drawers in a luxuriously shaped writing desk add so much more to its price as to make it unreasonable? Or is it already unreasonable—if we look at the shoddy workmanship inside? A sideboard is of very rare wood, well chosen and nicely finished: the doors are hung on cheap-looking hinges, the shelves fit badly, the drawers with their machine-made joints could be in a sugar-box. Remember: this is expensive, exclusive furniture with a reputation behind it.

I may be cranky, but such inconsistencies baffle me. I used to think it was because of an inexcusable lack of pride. Lately I'm not so sure. Many craftsmen can do better work—if people will only ask them to. People are not asking craftsmen to do better work because they no longer know enough about what that work might then be. This is sad. As a result, many craftsmen—I think this is especially true of those who work in wood—are becalmed. Somewhere between the mass-produced product and its honest opposite, we are confused.

And whose fault is that, one might ask.

The answer, if it comes, could cause a disturbance. Which is why some of us stay outside the competition, and go on being amateurs.

To me, sanding is *not* a way to express sensitivity with wood, even less a sign of true skill. It isn't the best—most direct—way to bring out delicate and clear shapes, but often an excuse for not being able to do so with a light touch of fine tools.

To be aware of this it is no doubt necessary to have experienced closely objects of another sort. Objects where everything is somehow, if not delicate, then clear. Surfaces have depth and luster: lines, edges, and corners are definite and in focus. They tend to be doughy when we use sandpaper, even with the best of intentions. The very nature of sandpaper—used with or without a pad, tends to press forth shapes, to knead them, rather than to outline, or underline them as well-used cutting tools do.

We can question the slight unevenness left by a plane or a chisel. Done wrong, it is an effect, yes. But there is something else there if we do it well: a clear shimmer, edges not circle-round, nice bevels. Often the scratches under an oiled or waxed surface tell us that someone has sanded here: With coarse paper first because he or she used machines and tools in a way that called for coarse sanding; then with finer paper, and lastly with fine—in the hope that each would erase the marks of its predecessor. Well, they did not. To me, sandpaper means a distance between the craftsman and his wood: using it, I can't feel the wood as I do with cutting tools. This is terribly frustrating, since my fingertips—even more than my eyes—tell me about what I am doing and also how I'm doing it. This fingertip communication is undoubtedly more vital to certain woodworkers than to others. Oh, we do need to see, to link eye and intuition, to be able to guess and then observe our efforts as they occur. But all the time our fingertips should be asking questions. Not merely confirming what we already know, or think we know—but asking questions: exploring edges, caressing surfaces, feeling their way along the curves.

Truly, I do believe that some of us, with our fingertips, keep a special eye on ourselves and our work!

3. DETAILS OF CABINETMAKING

COOPERED DOORS

Softly rounded surfaces appeal to me. They seem more natural and friendly than do flat or angled ones; after all, how often do we encounter a *live* surface of wood that is absolutely flat? Certainly not on an air-dried plank left nearly as the drying affected it, or on one that is hand-hewn. Nor on most old wooden objects. Indeed, with flatness comes what one might call the beginning of indifference.

I like to work with soft surfaces and subdued patterns in wood: coopered doors and the cabinet shapes they call for is my favorite way of doing this. When I discover an odd plank or two, and my attention has dwelt on a particular part of it, I am apt to imagine a curved door that will in turn result in a cabinet. Often there is something about that wood which I feel wants to be a curve: it has started, and needs only a little help. A door, yes; convex or concave, we will have to wait and see which— but a nice soft curve either way.

In some coopered work we see, the shapes remind us of a half-barrel with faceted staves, or a strange beetle: the shapes are carefully designed and their angles engineered to the purpose, interesting but somehow constructed they are; the wood is a color, and shapes have been given to it: it's been told what to say and do.

But here perhaps is a way to agree with what you imagine the wood wants. This is a searching. Since I have gotten into such work, the prospect of returning to it each time I find a "beginning" in a plank or planks is ever more exciting. It is as if, having done it before, I know better the challenge and promise and satisfaction that awaits me if only I go about this carefully enough. Carefully: by now I don't want to do it any other way. Even when I'm elated at the discovery of a very special piece of wood.

On the basis of what we already know: we can book-match, or else work across a whole width that corresponds to our door. A plank can be wide enough, flitch cut and containing all we want of color and pattern—or it might be nar-rower, quarter- or random sawn, and catch our eye with *part* of something that can be opened up, matched, and used—if we handle it with care. Once more keep in mind: if the rings are nearly vertical and the coloring calm, book-matching is less complicated; with the rings flat or nearly so, the matching becomes perilous, the patterns and shadings in the two halves balance only when first opened—after that they "leave" one another, causing disharmony.

For me it is more interesting to work with a plank already wide enough, one with the hint of a curve and a fanciful balance (but not exact symmetry) of pattern. As I later plane the curves this pattern will change, yes, but unlike the book-match, it will do so harmoniously. I can predict changes, follow them, and adopt the final shape and very character of the piece to how my door develops.

If our stock is, say, twelve inches wide and the bandsaw takes a six-inch depth, we can first divide the stock in two and re-saw each part to a suitable thickness. This will be 3/4 or 7/8

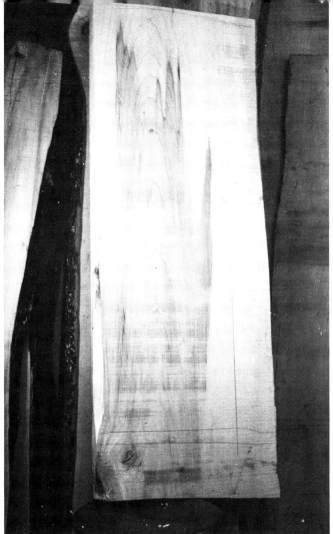

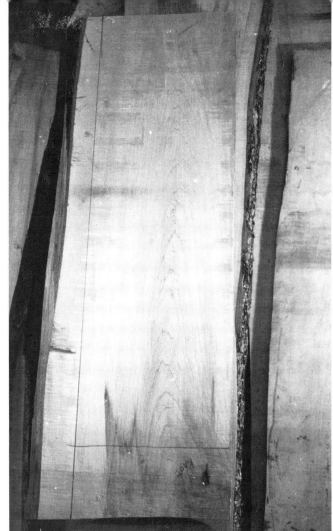

Beginning of a coopered door. Section of a two-inch-thick plank of Swedish maple about fourteen inches wide. There is a considerable amount of heart pattern on one side, and only a trace on the other. Knot and checks at bottom, top edge sawn above tip of heartwood color. When re-sawn to thickness, the pattern on the resulting surfaces will be somewhere between those now visible. There are then three alternatives to choose from: (1) very little heartwood, (2) about half the surface a darker pattern, and (3) an original outside of the plank with its greater amount of heartwood; in this case chosen as the outside of the door. Note: as this surface is worked (planed to shape) the dark parts will *decrease* slightly, whereas on the inside of the door, they will tend to lengthen with each cut of a hollow plane.

119

inch for a door 2 or 2 1/2 feet high. Keep in mind: you will want to joint the sawn surfaces smooth, and you'll be hand-planing the surfaces to a curve later on—so *the final thickness of your door will be less than you may first imagine.*

The curve of a mild, pleasant door is slight—about 3/4 inch on a width of eleven or twelve inches. Such a shape is not only pleasing, but also fairly easy to achieve: the work of beveling and gluing is not a great problem. Later on we can try more curved surfaces, even extreme ones that are almost a half-round if we so wish: for these we must use another method of gluing: since the pressure along a joint should be *at right angles to the glued surface*, we will need to have wood blocks or cleats along the various pieces as we glue them to one another.

To begin with, practice on a lesser curve. In many instances these gentle shapes are more subtle and rewarding to do, they suit the suggestive pattern of wood better and lead us to delicate details in the rest of the piece.

Doing a twelve-inch-wide door you will want to cut the stock lengthwise into six pieces: though not always; you can use four, or if the pattern is very subtle along the middle part, five so as not to make a cut just there. If at first you are unsure of yourself, and it is an advantage to make fewer cuts for the sake of keeping a pattern undisturbed, *then remember to add to the thickness,* since you will be hollowing-rounding each piece more to obtain the final shape.

If you decide on six widths, these need not be 2 inches wide each. In fact, it is an advantage to have them wider towards the middle: these two 2 1/2 inches, the next pair 2 inches, and the outer pair 1 1/2 inches each.

The reason for this is that if you make them equally wide and use the same bevel, you get an arc-of-a-circle curve. To me this curve lacks real interest, it hasn't the nice tension of a curve which increases (tightens) at its outer

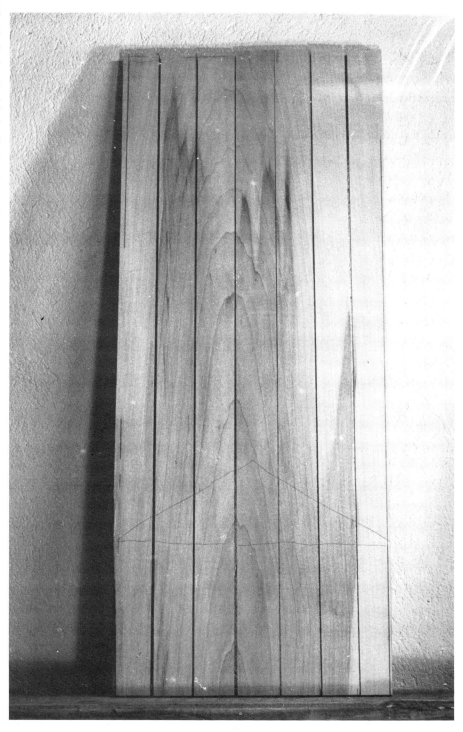

ends. With successively narrower widths you can use the same or nearly the same bevel—and obtain a shape that is more alive and intriguing.

Another way to achieve this result is to cut the pieces all to the same width and then bevel each pair differently: the middle ones less, the others successively more. A disadvantage of the "even-width" method is that in planing the outer pieces to a tighter curve we tend to make our door thinner here.

I usually feel there is a rela-tionship between the wood I've chosen—its texture and shadings —and the final shape of my door. The one illustrated is maple. It came from a flitch cut about half-way out from the middle of a log. There were four planks to begin with—most of an old log, all of them with bad cracks. I don't as a rule keep wood that has so many faults in it; because my shop is small, I try to bring in only usable pieces. But with maple the faults and the most beautiful surprises often go together.

Here there were fractures at the base and some long cracks at the other end: but between these I stumbled onto some-thing fine. The heart color was like little wisps of smoke, or tufts of grass coming up through the mauve sapwood, almost swaying as it seemed: there was a light space above before the nearest crack. The pattern of the fragile tips was complete and unharmed, a silhouette with an area of light sky behind and above.

This matter of pattern and how one reacts to it is all-important: it sets the tone of the whole piece. I had the feeling that if all those grass-tips hadn't been unharmed, if a crack up there had forced me to cut off the longest of those tips—all would have been lost. It's as if you saw a blade of grass swaying, then snipped off the tip—everything is changed.

So there was this pattern. I chose the side pieces to balance it as one viewed the cabinet from various positions: there's a mean-ing in the choice, with more heart-color on the side piece where there is less color on the nearest part of the door—and vice versa on the other side.

It's all a guessing, looking closely, and being lucky. An-other time with another wood, the entire result—shape, pro-portions, details—will be differ-ent. That's what makes the work so enjoyably exciting.

Pattern of side pieces chosen to balance with the door—which will usually be seen with one of these sides showing at a time.

121

If you can, allow a bit (two or three inches) on the length of the finished door because as you saw, bevel, and then joint the pieces there will be a small loss of width, and with this comes a slight staggering of the pattern and grain along each joint. So if you want a perfectly "whole" door you need to shift the pieces somewhat, slide them up or down to correct these discrepancies. And only a bit of extra length can make this possible. This is important if you want a truly fine door. When you make a thing like this that is almost but not quite perfect, a little imperfection becomes all too obvious; a detail only slightly amiss draws the eye like a blot on a page.

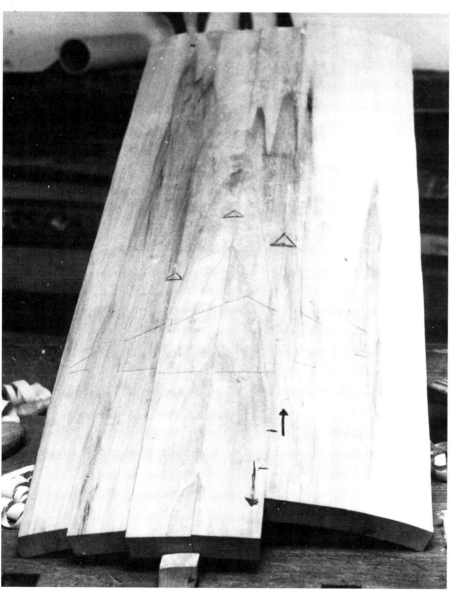

Door finally glued. Note how some pieces have been shifted to correct change or "loss" of pattern due to jointing.

You can make the first part of the bevels carefully on a jointer, though I prefer a hand-plane even here. Use small cuts. If the door is to be concave, watch out! You will be beveling at the front of each piece—the effect on pattern and grain is greater now than if it were a convex shape. The rest of the jointing you do entirely by hand; I use my favorite long plane—which I must first tune.

A joint should not be open at the ends before pressure: no, not even a little bit. As the opposite of this, you've heard about springing joints, planing them so they at first allow a bit of light through along the middle. Well, that's right—but the tendency is to be heavy-handed about it, and dip too much. If you do spring the pieces, it should be a feeling rather than a measure, noticeable only to you. A friendly rule is that *no two pieces should be forced together against their wishes: you should be able to press them tight together with your hands before gluing.*

You know—yet I must repeat it—a little glue and a little pressure is what gluing is about, at least in this case. We do not put clamps directly against the door parts, but use fairly narrow (1 1/2 inches) wood strips between these and our work. I round the outer edge of these strips on a slight arc to help them adjust more evenly to the curve of the door and the pressure against the various bevels.

Usually I "build" the door in two halves, gluing first two pieces of each and then the third—and finally do the middle joint. A small spring clamp at the ends of a joint will help keep them flush there, the rest you coax into place: with not too much glue the wood will quickly settle as the glue takes hold. Mark the pieces, watch them like a hawk for any wrong shift or slide: such misplacements affect the pattern and lessen the final thickness of the door. With the last joint especially there will be a tendency to buckle. Practice clamping, use clamps on both outside and inside, the outside ones can rest directly on the edge of the last joint, thus pressing it down as well as together. *Be sure the pressures balance and the joint is tight on both surfaces!* Have a lamp handy so you can look at the underside to check this.

Beveling edges and gluing parts of coopered door.

Rough-shaping two glued pieces at a time is handy—and will reveal any slight fault in the wood or the glue joint.

Planing the outside of the door to first rough shape.

To saw apart and re-do a joint is complicated and unnerving work, especially if the door is good and you are on the verge of spoiling it—as well you may, doing this kind of surgery. Time spent doing each step right is a good investment. Besides, you feel better knowing the work is going well.

Piece by piece we build a door. Always towards the end of the gluing-up I have this feeling of anticipation: I can hardly wait to start planing it to shape. Besides my flat planes I have six or seven rounded ones, each different and as carefully made as any other: with these I can work the inside shape of a door right down to the last light touches—after which I leave the surface this way, with the traces of the work itself there

for others to discover by eye and by touch. The same on the outside: I plane this, first to an approximate shape and then, after the cabinet is almost ready and the door fitted, I do the final polishing with one of my best planes.

Doing this work of shaping I experience a physical sensation of controlled strength: there is some rough hollowing out and rounding when I feel strong and warm and good, as though I'm climbing a mountain that I know—I've been on it before, but from another side.

Sometimes the door wants to remain curved only the one way, coopered as it is. Another time it shows just the slightest hint of a compound curve, being sprung outward along its length. Maybe only an eighth of an inch,

and yet it's there, a swelling so gentle one can hardly see it. I may add a trifle to it as I plane, and watch the pattern slowly change. It's a strange feeling, working with such small differences, such nuances. Like trying to bring forth an elusive intention in a low-tone, simple sculpture.

Will anyone notice it?

Hard to say. It isn't obvious, this curve-on-a-curve. Sometimes I look at a finished piece with someone who says he likes it. Can you see something special about the door, I'll ask. Special? It has a pleasant curve. *That* way, yes, but can you see anything more? I am sort of on edge now, wanting this other curve to be noticed. Don't you see it? No. And then I point out the lengthwise curve or spring, and tell about it, how small it is. Yet so important, I almost insist.

My explanation detracts rather than adds. One can start an academic or philosophical discussion about this subtlety—and only get farther away from a simple truth: to really see is to comprehend, intuitively and directly. Yanagi, as quoted by Bernard Leach, puts it so well: "Seeing directly constitutes a direct communication between the eye and the object. Unless a thing is seen without mediation, the thing itself cannot be grasped. . . ."

Final surface of door with "hand-friendly" traces of very fine plane worked with the grain of this hard maple.

As a cabinetmaker, I might include touch in the word seeing. Still the truth is unchanged: we have to *sense*, and react to the essence of the work.

Making a coopered door, you will also be involved with the rest of the piece; the final proportions, shadings and other details stem from the door, really. It affects the shape and position of the sides, the way the top and bottom pieces are—with the grain and formed edges relating to what the door calls for. It's a way of composing a piece, this, a game of now it's wrong, now it's right. I enjoy it, and, I must admit, hope to win a modest reward.

Various doors result in different solutions of the cabinet-case itself. A concave door almost always wants softly rounded sides set a little inward—otherwise the corners will be too sharp. A convex door can get along with flat, right-angled sides, though slightly curved ones may be even better. Much depends on the kind of wood: the colors, texture, mood of it.

On a concave cabinet the top and bottom pieces should give a sense of finely balanced downward and upward sweeps, respectively, accentuating the basic shape as we experience it. With a convex shape the opposite is true; we strive in all these de-

tails to achieve a feeling of oval.

As a rule I cut the door to size before doing the case: I find it less risky this way. I set up the door on my workbench or maybe the band-saw table—at roughly the height it will later be, on a wall—and I try different side pieces, with a strip above and

below representing the top and bottom pieces. I don't trust myself, I can't see things three-dimensionally on paper. So now I look, and look again at the mockup in different ways. I make a guess, knock on wood. And that's it; I cut the door to that length.

Cabinet of solid English brown oak with top and bottom pieces overlapping the sides, and shaped as desired. Cabinet sides are slightly curved, and set at an angle to "soften" the front corners.

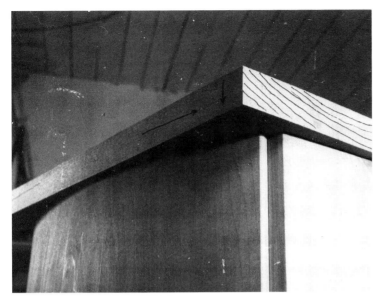

Choosing top and bottom pieces so as to obtain grain pattern congenial to convex curved shape of front. Even when the grain is subdued, the pattern is there.

As for the case itself, dovetails are a pleasant touch if the wood is light and the patterns are very simple, with perhaps a mere flick of color on the door. With more definite shadings, and wood that is not altogether delicate, you can keep the case simple by doweling it—especially when you want the sides curved, or set at a certain angle. Made this way our case can have subtle shadings along the top and bottom pieces, lines and shapes that enhance and enclose the surfaces with their colors.

Almost any interesting door will consist of sensitive hand-and-eye shapes—with the result that often the outer edges will not be exactly parallel: there is apt to be a slight wind to the door. You can't always correct it by planing without spoiling the door itself, since its thickness will be much affected. Don't let this discourage you! Try to make your door fairly straight, but if it isn't—*compensate any small wind in the door by trimming the cabinet sides—towards two opposite corners—until the door fits properly*. Do this when you first put the case together, before you determine the exact position of the hinges. And, of course, before you do any gluing!

We learn as we go along. Though some of our methods may not sound very professional, they are a result of experience, and a living part of our work.

The finished cabinet.

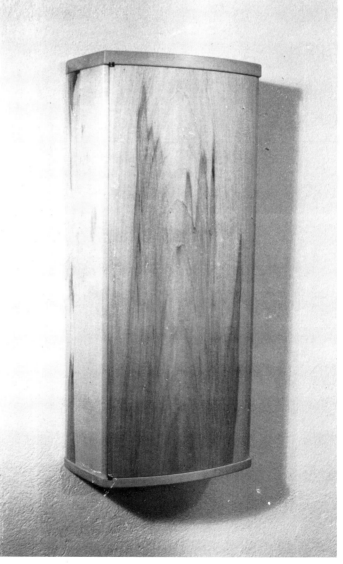

DOWELING

There is a lot of misunderstanding about doweling. While it is a widely used method in industry, rather little is known about it among craftsmen, at least in America; in Europe it is more commonly used. Because doweling is not visible as a joint, some craftsmen tend to be suspicious of it. When we use this technique without proper knowledge we use it badly, with bad results that increase our doubts.

By its nature, doweling is not convincing; the eye does not see how this joint is put together, and there is no pattern there to reassure you that those pieces of wood will stay together. When done right and used in a sensible relationship to the piece; to its character and its aims, doweling is a very good way of putting cabinets and even chairs together. It *is* primarily a commercial or production way of joining pieces, which I suppose is a part of our prejudice against it. Though most chairs on the market and a lot of the cabinets are doweled, and many of them stay together for years and years. They get scuffed and dingy and their surfaces become unpleasant so that we finally get tired of them and perhaps throw them away, but those are other faults; usually the doweled joints themselves are strong because they are well done on very accurate jigs.

Doweling. Solid wood piece with desired shadings along slightly overlapping top and bottom edges. Indian laurel.

The cabinetmaker's use of doweling should always be a matter of judgment. If you are making a seaman's chest that is going to be thrown downstairs or onto a ship, or a solid wood piece where other joints, visible and decorative, would be better, then use other joints. I do not think a seaman's chest should be doweled; it should be dovetailed. But a cabinet case can be doweled, especially if it is going to be a wall cabinet, and it will last for generations. One reason for choosing to dowel is visual, the character of the piece we are making. By doweling the case you can achieve a definite and fine-lined character; you get a visible top and bottom piece that can be made to protrude as you wish beyond the sides to give a horizontal outline at these extremities. You can do all sorts of nice things with these horizontals. You are free to bevel as you wish, to polish the end grain beautifully, to play with touches such as little roundings, and achieve the shadings which will emphasize the shape of the piece itself—lending it a very special air. Dovetailing, in contrast, is rather binding, since then the sides will probably be flush with the top and bottom pieces. All too often this results in a naked, stripped-down effect. You can put the carcase together with a false top and bottom on the inside and then add outer pieces, yes, but that is a complicated method and not always desirable. In many cases it is awkward, too, and there is a chance that the outer pieces will warp and crack away from the inner pieces which are dovetailed. And then, of course, the appearance of the cabinet is definitely limited by the fact that the sides are flush with the top and bottom, and there is this

pattern of the joints which, however pleasing, is not always appropriate; it lacks elegance in some respects, since it almost always has a rustic air.

Although I myself do not often work with surfaces that are veneered, they should be mentioned here in connection with doweling. On a fine bandsaw like mine it is possible to saw veneer 3/32 inch thick from solid stock; that is, from a chosen part of *the same wood you will use for the rest of the piece*. This I do on a few occasions, and the resulting veneer is so evenly sawn that I need not even surface it before gluing. The thickness, not over 3/32 inch, *allows me to work the wood as wood*—which some of the commercial veneers can hardly be called in these days of microthin cuts and the whole almost clinical process of using such veneers. With edge-gluings that allow for pleasant roundings, I have surfaces which are as fine as I want them: they can be polished with a plane, oil-finished or waxed—and they are alive, real wood. Here doweling is most handy as a way of putting carcases, small boxes and other pieces together. One can again work with fine shadings and proportions—but now, without the end grain being visible, these details are even more subdued and refined—if we so want them in a certain piece.

Doweling. Showcase cabinet with profiled top piece. Sides, top to bottom, are of veneer band-sawed from the same piece of wood as the rest of the cabinet, and finished with edges suitable to allow for subtle shapes desired. Maplewood.

131

Whether with your own veneer on a suitable wood core, or using only solid wood, you are working with horizontal and vertical lines, with overlappings and shadings, all sorts of subtle effects. Doweling frees you to do this. In certain situations doweling can be the best solution because of the judgment and sensitivity with which it has been used. It is, in other words, a way to add flexibility to your work on certain occasions.

The whole secret of doweling, and it is somewhat of a secret because of lack of common knowledge, is accuracy. You must be absolutely accurate. Some of us imagine we can make a jig and hold it against the piece to be drilled and then casually drill these holes. We can try, but the result will probably be a disappointment because the torque of the drill itself, *and a number of human factors,* result in holes that are not as accurate as they should be. A little bit here, a little bit there, and we've lost it; a sixty-fourth and a thirty-second and the whole thing gets out of hand; we have lost the very exactness that is the essence of making this joint. *This is definitely a case where it pays to do everything right, to take the extra time of making the jig, and of doing each step perfectly.* This way, doweling becomes an easy, not unpleasant, and very useful part of our cabinetmaking.

To do this kind of work we need a suitable electric drill and a stable horizontal surface on which to rest our work, this surface needs to be adjustable in relation to the drill or vice versa; we can raise and lower the drill itself, for instance. A fine simple machine for this purpose is the horizontal mortiser—just the basic machine without any special feed adjustments or other finesse. A poor man's version can be set up according to resources and inventiveness: it can consist of anything from a small portable drill mounted on a wooden stand, to a stable motor with a fine chuck and an adjustable rest made of metal. Such a set-up takes rather little floor space. It is absolutely essential for doweling. Besides this, it is a most useful piece of equipment when it comes to making mortises.

Fine fluted dowels are available in various sizes. However, they are not a hobby item, and are not likely to be found in the store around the corner; most of us are apt to end up with plain, smooth dowel stock in lengths of three feet or so, which is available in woodworker's supply shops and hobby shops. Simply lay the long piece of dowel on your bench, place a rough woodrasp diagonally on the dowel and roll the dowel along the bench with it. This will produce a series of scores which, although they don't hold the glue as well as do flutes, nonetheless increase the holding power of the dowel. Cut the dowels to suitable length.

Now you have to choose a drill that will give you a tight fit, even on end grain. I point out this matter of end grain because a drill which produces a good fit cross-grain tends to make a hole in end grain that is a bit too large. Another point to keep in mind is that though you will have a jig, you still want a drill that really centers and does not drift, causing oval holes and general inaccuracy. What you want is a drill that tends to center itself and cuts very clean even in end grain. There are cabinetmaker's drills available with a lip and a center spur but these come only in limited sizes and often are not very high quality. A simple way to make what we in Europe call a cabinetmaker's drill is to regrind an ordinary straight-shank metal drill. This may sound complicated but it really is not; with a small grindstone in an electric drill you can easily produce drills with a sharp center spur and very sharp, clean-cutting edges. When ground right this type of drill will cut beautiful holes in any kind of grain, producing a perfect result and crisp shavings. Once you have practiced grinding drills this way, and done a few, and achieved the first successful result, you will want to use these kinds of drills more and more on wood. With better and better results. As to sizes; try the dowel and the drill together, and achieve a snug fit in cross-grain as well as end grain. This usually means the drill size will be just under the diameter of the dowel itself, and here again the reground metal drills are an advantage because they are available in a great number of different sizes.

The jig is simply a piece of straight wood squared off and with a plywood or a thin solid wood heel on one end which will correspond to the back side of our cabinet or box or whatever. As an example; if the width of the area we are to dowel together is six inches there will probably be from six to eight dowels. Space these according to your judgment, evenly if you choose, but preferably a bit closer together at the front and back edge, since you do need a bit more holding power there than in the middle of the joint. The short heel at the back should be absolutely square with the rest of the jig. It is well to remember that the holes for dowels should be drilled along the center of the end pieces, and not near the inner or outer edge.

It is an illusion to think that you can hold the jig in place simply by hand as you do the drilling. Therefore, obtain a nice thin brad or perhaps a hardened nail that is used for hanging pictures on walls, and drill a hole in the jig somewhere near the middle area that is a snug fit for the small nail or brad. This is very important, since with a tight fit and the brad driven in properly the jig will not slip.

A straight-shank steel drill reground (shaped) for use in doweling, etc.

Regrinding drill-tip. Edge of wheel should be *slightly* rounded.

All the parts you are to drill and assemble should be properly marked. This may sound obvious, yet it is amazing how often we forget to mark the pieces or, when we do mark them, achieve results that are confusing. We use A, B, C, and 1, 2, 3, and X, Y, Z—all sorts of codes that may or may not work out properly for us, but usually do not. It is a puzzle to me why the classic cabinetmaker's mark of the pyramid or triangle is neglected, because when it is used properly, it is infallible. Once you get used to it and begin to think in terms of inside-outside, front-back, top-bottom, then this mark is so clear in its message that there is no room for confusion. The illustrations show how this works. *We determine whether we shall use the inside or the outside of our side-pieces as a point of departure; that is to say whether the most important thing for us is the exact placement of the outside surface or inside surface.* Then we mark the pieces accordingly. We put the piece to be end-drilled on the table of our circular saw or joiner, place the jig against it and drive home the brad—making sure the heel is tight against the back edge. Check and recheck this. Think through the way the piece is going to be put together, the relationship of the jig to the surfaces, and the measurements that are most important, before you fasten the jig! Drive home the brad deep enough to hold, but not all the way; you will be removing it as you change the jig from one end of the piece

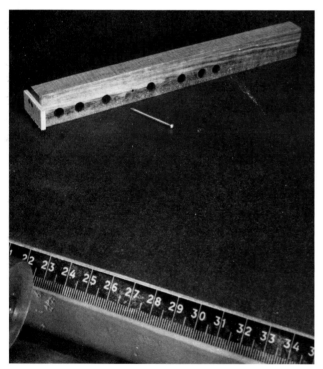 

Jig for doweling. The brad is to hold
it in position when drilling.

The classic cabinetmaker's pyramid-marking: when used right, it is absolutely reliable.

to another. Drill carefully and steadily, holding the jig (even though it is nailed) firmly with your hand. Drill a little deeper than the length of dowel which is to go into the sides or the end-grain pieces. If you do not drill deep enough, then when you drive the dowel in for keeps the glue will run and make the work messy, so allow a little space at the bottom for excess glue and for the dowel to be able to "breath" a little. Before you put the dowels into the parts with the end grain (which usually contain a larger part of the

length of the dowel than do the cross-grain top and bottom pieces), countersink the holes a little. Then decide how much of your dowel is going to go into cross-grain pieces; the top and the bottom for instance, or the short ends of a box or a case, and allow approximately that much dowel to protrude. You can drive the dowels home with the help of a small block which corresponds to the thickness that you want to allow for, or you can insert the dowel a bit less deep than needed and then saw the protruding ends to an even length with the help of a strip of wood.

Prepare for gluing by getting together all you need; glue, a little piece of thin dowel with which to coax the glue into the holes, pieces of rag, a proper hammer, and a little spacer block to use as a stop when tapping the dowels into place. Work carefully and methodically. Blow out extra shavings or crumbs from the holes, put in enough glue but not too much, be careful in every respect, even to the extent of checking and rechecking that the ends of the pieces into which you have drilled holes are square and true. Glue the dowels properly, and then set these pieces aside.

Drilling for dowels in end-grain of cabinet sides.

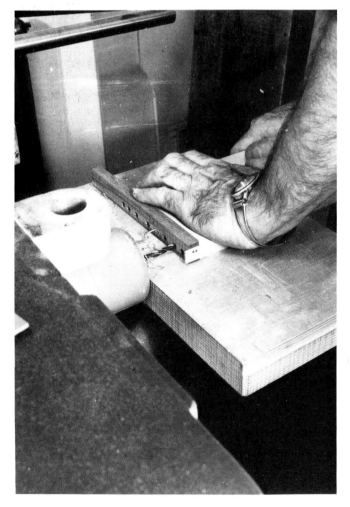

Countersinking to remove burr and also to allow for particles of dowel which might be pressed here when gluing.

Gluing in dowels after checking that
ends of cabinet pieces are flat and
true.

Now you are going to use the jig on the top and bottom pieces themselves. There is the edge of the jig which you had turned *down* as you drilled the first holes: this edge is now your line of orientation; you will use it flipped to correspond with "in" or "out" to achieve the exact relationship between top, bottom and sides that you want. Mark the top and bottom pieces carefully, place the jig there with the heel tight against whatever is the back edge, and then clamp it firmly in position. See that your drill is of the right size, use this in a small portable electrical machine or even a hand-drill. *Do not drill without a wooden stop on that part of the drill shank which is beyond the depth that you want.* Check and recheck this! Remember; you want the hole in the cross-grain of the top and bottom piece to obtain the maximum holding power. But if you do not want an accident you don't drill all the way through. So check this wooden stop, which can be a little block of wood that you have drilled and placed on the shank of the drill, or a piece of thick dowel with which you have done the same. Check the depth against the jig itself before you proceed. Drill the holes carefully, holding the drill vertically, so that you really are drilling all the holes straight down neatly without wobbling too much. This whole thing is a matter of accuracy, and of thinking clearly. The tendency is to be too much in a hurry because you are nearing the point where you are going to put the case

together and look at it for the first time. But do be patient; think of the consequences of each mistake, and avoid making it.

After drilling and slightly countersinking the holes in the top and bottom comes the proof of the care and accuracy with which you have worked: You should have a good strong fit and be able to tap the piece together without undue violence. When you have it together dry, consider what should be done next: maybe a door that needs to be fitted, or the back piece; also how the interior of the case will be. *Think in terms of several steps, don't take one little detail at a time and then knock the case apart and do a small bit of work on and put it together and think about the next little step.* Try to go through as much of the process in your mind as possible at one time. I usually take a chip of wood or a piece of paper and jot down the various things that need to be done, such as planing the back of the piece flush all around early so that whatever machining need be done there later, a rabbet or a groove, will be accurate. Consider the overhang of the top and bottom in relation to the doors or door, the shadings with which you will want to mark various details, the bevels you will make. All these things are important. And since you are making something that you hope will be graceful and interesting and neat, you do want to do each part of the work at the right time. If there are to be partitions in the box or cabinet, you need to make the grooves for

these before you glue the piece together. There will be holes for shelf pegs, or a recess for a latch or hinges. We'll think about how we shall finish the inside of our piece. All these things must be done before it is too late—not just before it becomes impossible but before doing them becomes more difficult than it should be. That way you are apt to make mistakes and produce a piece not as neat and clean and appealing as you hoped it would be. We want all the time to work towards success, towards achieving the result we strived for, really, and not to have to say: "I was in too much of a hurry to glue the piece together, and I forgot to do this or that; I had to do it later, and it didn't turn out so well because I just couldn't get in there to do it right. . . . The time we take to think and rethink is time saved, not lost. Once we get into this habit we develop a step-by-step logic which we use without any strain and this adds to the ease and enjoyment with which we work.

As to the gluing itself: I nag a lot about that. One thing is worth repeating: *put the piece together dry with all clamps and blocks to be sure that it goes together tight*, is straight and true, square where it needs to be square, that the holes for the dowels are deep enough. Check your lists of what needs to be done, make sure that it has all been done properly. *Don't trust yourself.* I think a basic rule of cabinetmaking is to mistrust oneself and recheck everything. When you are actually going to glue, remember, of course, to

Drilling for side pieces which here are to be set at slight angle inward toward front. Note piece of cardboard between heel of jig and piece to be drilled: this compensates for the change of angle (departure from ninety degrees), and will lessen the differences at the back of the pieces when fitted together. When you work with right angles this is simpler—the heel of the jig fits all back edges tightly.

A good fit.

Cabinet (English oak) doweled, with final shaping yet to be done.

have what you need, the rags, the blocks again, those clamps which you have tried before. Everything properly set up. Very often a craftsman is alone in his shop when doing this kind of thing: if you have made a mistake, omitted something or not tried to clamp the piece together dry, then with the glue on you are apt to run into serious trouble when you least expect it and have no one to turn to for help. It is amazing how easy it is to spoil a week's work in just a few minutes. When you are tense and in a hurry you are apt to be violent, you rush after things, turn the piece over on its side or upside down, there is a bit of scrap on the bench that causes a dent, you drop something, put a clamp on crooked. One little error leads to another, your confusion increases until finally you are working in a destructive frenzy. Avoid this. Taking your time is a basic rule of this kind of work. Not enough glue is bad, but too much glue can also be a kind of disaster, spoiling that neatness you want so hard to keep. Using glue in the right way adds to your self-confidence, it helps you to work more calmly and, of course, it ensures a better result. I remember a woodworker who used to say, either as a joke or as a wry comment when we students were wiping out a lot of glue in corners and along edges and muttering to ourselves, "Well, at most it is supposed to seep just a tiny bit, you know. Now all this glue you are wiping up—what are you going to use it for? What will you do with it?" What

indeed. It does spread, it does leave its traces in little corners that you will never quite get into, corners that will not be quite as neat as if you had glued everything perfectly. So try to develop the habits which will lead to satisfaction, and keep the piece on the level you had set from the beginning. With luck, you may even surpass that level.

DOVETAIL JOINTS

How does one talk about dovetail joints without being a bore? After all that has been said and written on the subject, what can I add that's worth remembering? Not much. Dovetails are among the three or four kinds of joints we use the most. And let's admit it—the one we misuse the most. Hand-cut dovetails in a piece can easily become more important than the piece as a whole. Poor proportions, hurried work: but, man, look at those dovetails!

On the other hand, sometimes we avoid dovetails, simplify our construction to get around making these joints. After all, they are difficult to do, and take a lot of time. Even done badly they take time. In a competitive situation it is easier to use another joint: the dovetail is used where it advertises itself—and us—as on the front of a drawer. But back there under the fancy table or whatever, the same drawer is put together any old time-saving way; slotted, finger-jointed, even half-lapped. These are not always done badly: some professionals make fair joints, strong ones, with machines. Yet they have a definitely mechanical air,

at least for anyone who knows about such matters.

Those who want to convey another and more personal message, to be consistent about the quality of their work, use dovetails (like other joints) in the right place and in the right way. More often than not this consistency includes a lot of discipline: pulling yourself together and doing the thing, whatever the time and effort. Sometimes this is easy, at others it is not. Much depends on whether you are doing it for fun, so to speak, as an amateur—or whether you have to make a living as a cabinetmaker and are dependent upon finding people who will really appreciate, I mean even *evaluate*, fine points as a part of fine workmanship. There is a balancing line somewhere here, and it is very important to keep on the side of that line which is right for you.

For fun or as livelihood, dovetailing is detailed, methodical work. Monotony is not far away, not only in the process but also in the results. It's so easy to drift into too much method and not enough imagination. Or the other extreme: fantasy galore—at the price of skill and patience.

It's balance we want. Strong, interesting joints as part of a good piece of furniture. Joints we enjoy doing different ways at different times because we know we can do them, know how and with what to work.

In order to win freedom to use our imagination and do good work like this we need perhaps to feel there is a painless way of doing it. Not easy. Not for free—

that's no fun. But painless, without disharmony. A way we can look forward to. That is so crucial at times: we need to want to do the work, even when it is a bit uphill.

The process of dovetailing is fairly involved, and so are the tools we need here—if we care enough about the results to get past the generalities. If we excuse a lack of skill, or the failure to improve certain tools, by saying our work has an old-fashioned charm or grass-roots honesty, we may be fooling ourselves and someone else, too. We are avoiding the fact that we could do the work better, or easier, or both.

We balance our work upon what we are and how we live. Someone in a hamlet makes charming kitchen interiors of pine. Another person in another place works on the same level of honesty, but with pearwood—and even if the level is the same, the path is different: he feels the wood calls for exactness and refinement. He knows how to achieve these qualities, and he wants to do so, because it fits an idea and a feeling he has. Once he has come this far there is no way of going back without changing his whole philosophy, the way he lives. The naiveté of the villager would in this man be second-hand.

If we want to mark pearwood for a sensitive joint we need a marking gauge with a very fine tip. Whether it is the traditional all-wood gauge with its two sticks, head, and wedge that you tap so carefully in order to make an exact adjustment—or the common up-to-date model with a simple set-screw, the tip (or pin) has to be perfect.

Most marking gauges as we buy them have the tip protruding much too far. And it is shaped wrong: being simply pointed like the end of a nail. No wonder it scratches, goes astray and generally misbehaves. You want that

tip to protrude just a hair, hardly 1/64 inch. It can be half-moon shaped, with the inside edge parallel to the head and the outside sloping slightly, nicely rounded. And sharp, sharp. Experiment with this. If you think I advocate too short a tip, keep in mind: a mark made cross-grain goes deeper than you'd suppose. Wanting to get past the mark when finishing and fitting a drawer you can find yourself planing away too much and spoiling a good fit. This business of joints is all small details, you see.

Cabinetmaker's scribe, metal, of sort most readily available. Tip has been carefully shaped by user.

141

Before proceeding, let me try to clarify the terms I use regarding these joints. For reasons of language and habits I refer to the pins—that is the protruding parts of one half joint—as the dovetails. The recesses or openings into which these fit I call openings, though others may regard them as the dovetails. The accompanying sketch will, I hope, keep us clear of confusion.

No joint is better than the saw cuts that made it—this might remain a generalization, a cliché, unless we look into what it means for some of us.

Years ago, I was at a school with some fellows who were very cool and casual about—among other things—doing dovetails. You were supposed to sit side-saddle on your workbench, the piece you were cutting tucked under one thigh, and nonchalantly tap, tap as you cut the dovetails. When you sawed these it was the same: you had this bow saw (frame saw, we Europeans call it) and you used it with the same ease—squinted along the mark, and cut. Cool.

Well, a few of the chaps actually were good doing this. Even though the bow saw looked awkward, the blades we had in those days were excellent; thin-gauge, fine-toothed, wide, and straight, set just enough but not too much. Another point to note is that most of the so-called perfect joints, such as those in our apprentice pieces, were done in mahogany. Now mahogany, though it is regarded as a hardwood, isn't really hard. It has a lot of give-and-take, the parts of a joint adjust to one another. Then too the color of mahogany is rather neutral; it doesn't expose small faults as would maple or ash, for instance. Even with this help from the wood, our hotshots were not always all that casual; there was a bit of muttering, furtive glances, drawer parts with saw-cuts "left over." And maybe someone mixing glue into mahogany sawdust: very thin hide glue, and only a few drops but still. . . .

Later, when we had to make joints in pearwood or any other true hardwood that had no give, we discovered that being cool was not the whole answer. Cool or not, any little misstep in sawing or chiseling was there to stay.

At another school, recently, the experience was different. The program was new, most of the equipment had not yet arrived; we had to make do with the first tools we could get. We did simple exercises such as making dovetailed boxes. Most of the students were eager beginners; this was going to be fun. And it was. But some were frustrated: saw-cuts were out of line, chisels left bruises on the tapered openings for dovetails, the dovetails themselves leaned this way and that. When the boxes were put together the joints were not tight at the top and bottom. We had been a trifle unrealistic in our exuberance. The flat surface of our chisels was neither flat nor smooth, but bore the deep scratches of an all-too-efficient production method. We spent hours whetting away these flaws and others, struggling to the stage where the tools were just acceptable.

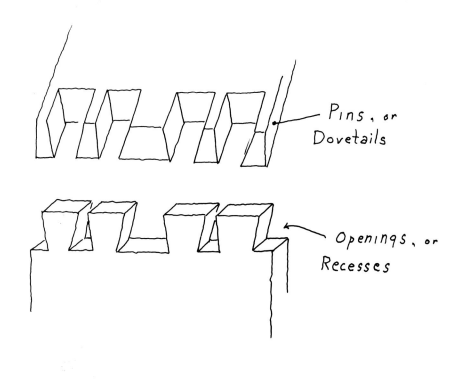

Pins, or Dovetails

Openings, or Recesses

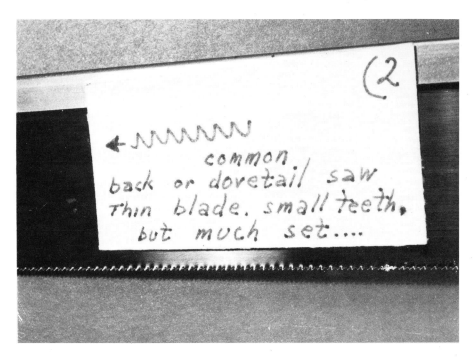

Some of the excess set was removed from the saws by clamping the cutting edge between two pieces of straight flat iron or steel—the spring-back after releasing the vise or clamps left the teeth set nearly right. They cut better than before but not well enough, not so we could relax and let the saw do the work. No, we still had to steer, press, tense ourselves. And even then the cut was apt to be something different than we had marked for.

Common type of dovetail saw. Teeth sometimes have too much set.

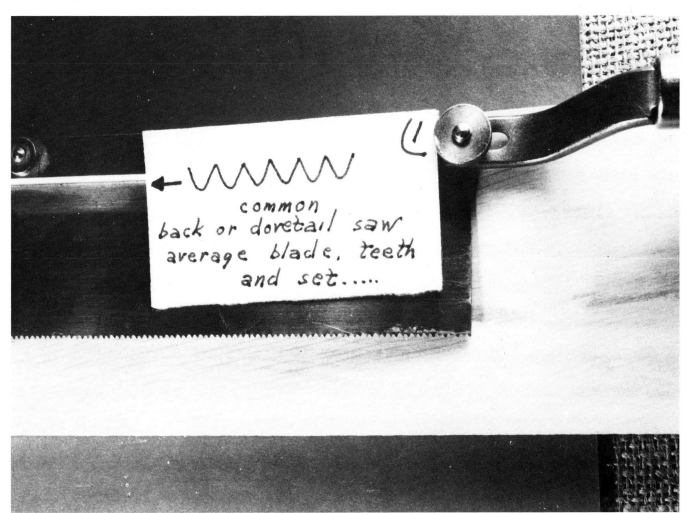

I had with me a pair of Japanese dovetail saws, and some of my old Swedish chisels—some of the tools I have lugged to and from America since 1969. We passed these around, using them to get the feel of these much used, finely tuned tools. For those who could see, the difference between a saw and a saw came to light. One saw skates around chattering before it starts, then weaves one way and another on the way down, bulldozing a path that's far too wide. A good saw listens to our intentions. It has a feel which I can only describe as right for my work—this means you'll need to find the saw or saws which suit you and *your* work. The Japanese ones come in different sizes for different purposes; they are produced for everything from cutting thin bamboo to building houses. I like them, and believe each is balanced to its purpose. And the logic of these saws is so beautiful: you hold a piece of thin metal in one hand, press the opposite end, and the piece buckles. Again: you pull instead of press—the piece becomes, and stays absolutely straight. Perhaps someone discovered this truth with a blade of grass, a thousand years ago.

Japanese saws (and chisels) may not be readily available, though their use is spreading. When you buy these tools, remember that there are several types of saws to choose from. *Special files are needed* to sharpen some of them: get the files before, not after, your saw becomes dull.

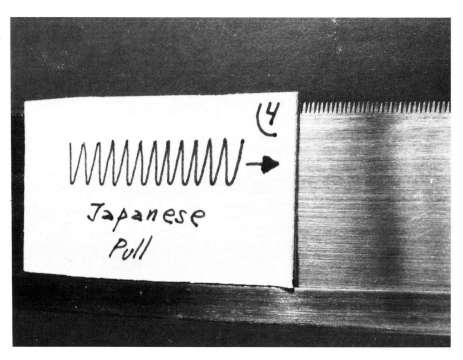

Japanese dovetail saws. Available in U.S.: there is a variety of sizes and types.

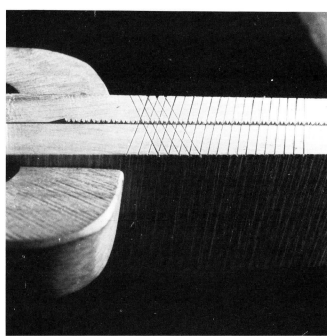

Saw-kerfs (cuts). The thin, even ones are from Japanese saws.

Sharpening a Japanese (or any fine-toothed) saw. The clamped-on hard-wood strips assure even bottoming of each tooth. Also, each series of file-cuts leaves its score (mark) on the wood: this serves as an orientation and saves eye-strain.

Special file for Japanese saws. Note the very low angle of the bevel on this file. The vise shown here is by Ulmia (available in the U.S.). It is well made and very useful.

Having to get along without the Japanese ones at the school, we found a straight-back dovetail saw made by Kuntz; blued thin steel, fine toothed. The back was not offset: when cutting joints we need to see well on both sloping cuts, along either side of the saw. After we removed the excess set the saw stopped its antics, and we could practice our cuts so as to control them. To start properly is half the battle, really, and here is where a saw that chatters and skids throws us off. The beginning of a cut is all-important not only because it determines the relationship of the cut to the mark, and thereby the fit, but also we want the *whole* joint beautiful, including the outside edge, where any unsteady start leaves its tell-tale signs. We imagine we will get past these polishing the piece, but often we do not.

In time we were working in close relationship to the marks we had made. We could both see and sense whether we were on a line, or just a hair inside it; where we should be when sawing the recesses. One simple hint led to another. To help get the dovetails themselves straight, marking was not enough: we could mark neat right angle lines and still saw askew. It did help to have an orientation: this is horizontal; this, vertical. So we clamped our piece in the bench-vise with the end exactly horizontal (we sighted against a door, windowsill, etc)—and then concentrated on making our cuts vertical. Marks became less important than the direction of our cut; we felt rather than saw that we were cutting straight and true. This lining up isn't foolproof; a saw can tend to drift one way or another, but it is a help. Besides: we don't have to stare and squint at those lines all the time.

Now we could pay more attention to finishing the cut on the scribe marks, not above or below. On; with the saw held level so we have the cut as it should be on both sides of the piece. We blow the dust from the kerf to see where we are (the thin Japanese saws especially leave a lot of fine dust in the kerf, and it is hard to see where the bottom of the cut really is). Watch this. Get used to your saw. You want the corners of each tenon neat.

We did get by with the saws we had. Although we could still wish for better ones, it felt good to know we had made the best of what was available.

Sawing well encouraged us to be optimistic about using our chisels. Though we had honed them, they had what might be called a standard bevel. They did cut, and we made some joints. But at the same time odd things were happening. Already after the first few blows of the mallet the inside edge of our cut—with the scribe mark—was pressed back a little; out of line, that is. And as we worked farther into the wood our chisel wanted to lean or tilt inward as it went down, after cutting from both sides we had an opening with its inside in a "V" that was not mild (as we knew it could be) but steep enough to worry us. The wood there had crumbled, and along the whole of our piece that out-of-line thing was evident: some of the cuts were more to the side of the mark, others less.

Chisel with usual standard bevel.

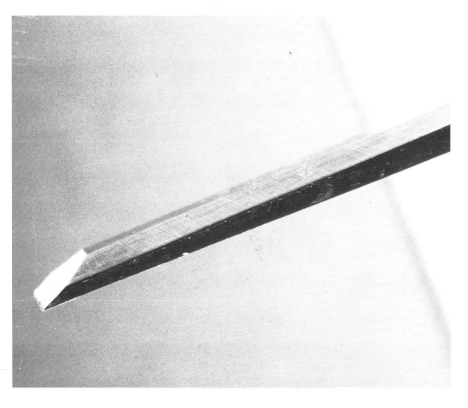

We were not entirely happy. When we cut the little openings for the tenons we had the same trouble—and a new one besides: the tapered openings that looked so promising when we sawed them were bruised at the edges where the back (or was it the side?) of the chisel had pressed. The chisel is supposed to be shaped to avoid this. We wet the wood to raise the grain into place —well almost—and kept going.

The joints, finally, were not bad. At the same time they could have been better: there was the uneven line of the dovetail openings, the corners where we had sawed along the scribe marks were not tight, either. Was the saw kerf really *that* wide? We had spent time doing the joint, it wasn't that we rushed it, and could blame the result on haste. Worst of all: we were not quite sure we'd do it better next time.

So we talked about this. About what is in the books and maybe some things not in the books, and about how we can use all this in a way that feels good.

You see, a chisel with the usual from-the-dealer bevel is not necessarily ideal for cutting fine joints. Theoretically it should not "lean" as it cuts; in practice it does just that, at least for most of us. Theoretically we shouldn't bruise the tapered openings as we cut across their inside; actually we do bruise them quite often, especially when they are for nice, thin tenons. When we can use a chisel quite a bit smaller than any given opening and we can tip our tool to one side or the other, the work goes fairly well. But with small and finely proportioned joints we haven't much leeway— a chisel just about fits our openings; the next two sizes are wrong either way. Some of us buy extra chisels and grind these to in-between sizes. Still, the smaller the dovetails, the more demanding the work.

I am often asked about cutting tools: where to get ones of the finest steel, what brand is best. Honestly, I don't know. It all depends on you and your work. On how much you care about the final sharpness that gives a clean cut: after all, what help is the finest steel if we are not eager to sharpen our tools perfectly and keep them that way?

The scale of work you do matters, too, as does the wood you use most—there is so much difference between working with bubinga, for instance, and pine or mahogany. Few chisels nowadays are consistently good or bad. I suspect that production methods change from year to year—or at least they seem to, judging by the way some cutting tools behave. Five years ago one Swedish manufacturer made a fine chisel; not only was the steel excellent, but the finish was good—you did not have to spend a day and a half whetting the one side flat; it was flat, and without the deep scratches which we all hate. Now the company is a part of a larger firm, a maker of wrenches, and the chisels show it. Or am I imagining things? At any rate; Bahco, Marples, Stanley, and others make chisels —your choice is as good as mine. Steel tends to be too hard or too soft; if you can find that in-between ideal smooth quality, you are lucky.

There are Japanese chisels available, too. These are beautifully made, expensive, with an extra-hard cutting edge. This edge, once you get it sharp, is gorgeous for paring: a 1 1/2- or 2-inch Japanese chisel, sharp, is a beautiful tool. On heavy work with hard wood it might chip, but with that light touch you can use such chisels in all sizes and for most purposes—if you can find and afford them.

Whatever chisels, or other tools for that matter, the final judgment is yours. And it must include how much or how little you care about any subtle difference, how much time and attention you are willing to devote to these tools—not just once in a while, but steadily. In other words, what these tools mean to you must be decisive for your choice of them.

Years ago I reground my chisels to a double bevel—a long gentle slope and then a short steeper one about the same as most cabinetmakers use. It took some doing, but afterwards and for a long time the cutting edge and short bevel needed only to be honed now and then. On the larger chisels, 3/4 inch and wider, this bevel can be slightly thicker, on the smaller sizes the long slope runs almost out to the tip.

Won't the edge chip and break easily? No. As long as you use it properly it will hold up just as well as a chisel ground any other reasonable way. By properly, I mean with the care and judgment it deserves, which, after you have worked to get it really fine, will be quite a lot. A part of the cutting

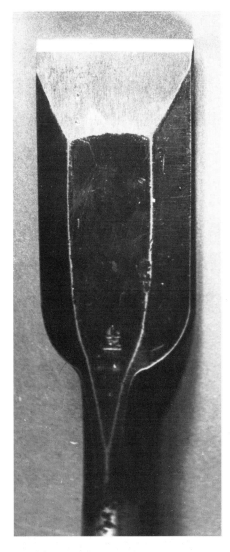

edge is at a normally used angle—it won't chip easier because the rest is sloping back out of the way. When anyone bangs into a piece of bubinga and the chisel-edge goes *trrt*, the resulting nicks are seldom over 1/32 inch deep. I assume we are talking here about modest or even small joints, work that is an attempt at refinement, that we can enjoy doing, and that isn't a struggle. We are not going to just whack away at it, we want to coax the chisel with sure, tireless taps—and then cut back. Some of us use our mallet on the cut-backs, others push the chisel. If it feels awkward to lay aside the mallet after each down cut, then use it lightly on all the cuts. Watch where you place the tip of your chisel—it is so easy to damage a small opening.

Cut lightly down: a chisel with a double bevel does not tend to pivot, but keeps the vertical direction in which you hold it—again provided you make small cuts. Form the habit of doing many small cuts instead of fewer large ones: this is the key to

cutting cleanly and well.

Too slow?

It all depends on what you want to do and how you do it. One fellow bangs away and gets things done. Another tap, taps—and he too, gets things done. The question is: on what level. What did the doing take, and what did it give?

Even if the pros scoff I will add this: when you find your own answers and the fine points of what you want to do, there will be results. Don't worry. On a sensitive quality level you'll get more done than many a competitive craftsman who seeks the easy way out.

You can't do some of the showy things they do? They can't ever do the refined things you will be doing.

I really believe this. I can't prove it, but I hope you will, because it is true. The deft, personal touch is not only more satisfying, but also more productive when it comes to doing fine work. One of the worst fallacies in crafts education is that this is not so, that finesse is only for dreamers.

What is finesse? I really don't always know, unless it is a level of refinement.

Well, when we have solved some of the problems with scribe, saw, and chisel, there is still the matter of cutting evenly along a fine line every time we need to do so. We can concentrate hard: this will help—until we get tired. However, I believe any non-mechanical aid that will enable us to be more sure of the results, and spare worry, is worth a try.

Chisel reground to double-bevel as described in text.

I have been using a guide as shown in the photo here. It's just a piece of hardwood with coarse sandpaper glued to the under-side, 1/16 inch or so in from the straight edges, which can be trued if need be without running into the grit. Have a lamp you can adjust so as to get the light as you want it; you need to see your scribe mark and the way the block follows it perfectly. Practice sighting in and then clamping the guide exactly in place: the edge of your chisel against it will also be on the mark. And then you simply relax, holding the chisel upright and tapping lightly with a smallish, nicely balanced mallet. Tap easily and cut on a low slope back. And again. The straight edge helps you to both follow the line and keep the down-cuts vertical. I do not think anyone need feel embarrassed using this aid, since it is an honest one that almost eliminates the possibility of mistakes. So if it suits you, use it—and be glad.

Only one detail remains before we have this matter of dovetails completely under control: to get a sure, tight fit at the outer edges (corners) of each joint. We have been sawing in along the scribe line there—with varied results: the risk of cutting inside the mark is a worry. So now one more hint. On the piece that will take the dovetails themselves, start cutting your recesses, including the outer ones, all along the guide block. But at the outside ones, do not cut through or even far down—simply start the cut and then leave it as a shallow notch on each side. Cut the other recesses free, remove the guide,

Straight-edged wood block with sandpaper glued to "down" side. An aid when doing dovetails.

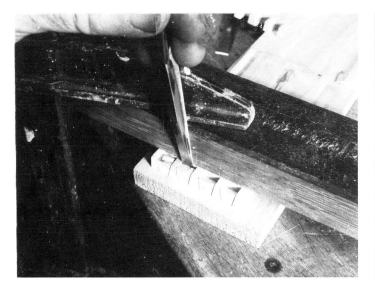

Dovetailing. Clean cuts leave neat, well-fitting parts.

flip the piece on edge in your bench vise, and very carefully cut a corresponding notch on each edge, coaxing the chisel on the mark and just barely tapping the first cut. Make a notch with a vertical inside edge that will provide a shoulder for your saw. Now, and only now, saw straight down along this and the adjoining notches. Your finished cut will be in line with the rest of the openings, though look closely— you may want to pare it a trifle since you have sawn not so much on the original scribe line as just outside it. This is a good habit: in marking, sawing, chiseling, you develop these tendencies of almost unconsciously keeping on the safe side of a line or a cut. It's not the same as intentionally making allowances, which tend to be too great and result in a lot of pick and poke with chisel and saw. No, I mean the tiny, almost imperceptible difference that keeps you on the safe side—but just. It's a feeling you develop if you care enough about what you do.

Steps in obtaining a tight fit at the ends (corners) of a dovetail joint.

151

Now there's the whole joint. And it is tight. You can look from above or from below and see that it is tight all the way. It is nice: in a cabinet or a drawer we like to have that tightness all along, front and back, everywhere. Not because we want to boast, but because this is the way we do it, and it leaves us at ease because we feel good about it. Boasting is for those who do such nice joints only part of the time.

The matter of making joints, dovetail or others, is one of method and exactness—and something more. That "more" is the logic and fantasy of our message.

The logic of it is, I believe, to think in terms of function and decoration—in that order—without being showy about either. It is so tempting to exploit joints, and let them compensate for deficiencies elsewhere in the piece. I don't necessarily mean that we calculatingly do this: rather, the fact that joints are a lot of work may, once we have them done and are perhaps tired, cause us to concentrate less on the remaining details of the work. But when we know we can do all the work well we feel more relaxed about it and it becomes easier to think from inside the piece and to weave together the how and why of what we do.

Fantasy isn't necessarily original ideas and unusual shapes. We could perhaps save a bit of its meaning for a less obvious expression: the sense of rhythm

One of the drawers in a maplewood cabinet.

and proportion in—among other things—joints themselves.

The function of a good joint is to keep pieces of wood together in a certain way. The decoration is most often a pattern which we know quite well by now, one that repeats itself. If this is so, then perhaps we can hope to do better. And I think we can. For instance: by habit (or training) cabinetmakers tend to divide a given space into equal distances when laying out dovetails. So does a machine. Instead, we could remember that the strain on a cabinet case, box, or drawer is greatest at the outsides (or corners) of each edge—the top and bottom of a drawer front, the front and back of a cabinet: that's where joints tend to let go. Not in the middle. By usage and because of how the air affects a piece, the tendency will be for it to warp, or break outward at the corners. Make this a

part of your thinking and instead of that even spacing, play with function and decoration as part of one another—respace the joints, put the dovetails closer together at the outside, where the strain is greatest, and let the space between them increase towards the middle. Try to weave together the spacing, the angles at which you cut the dovetails, how thick or thin these are. Relate all this to the wood you are using—and to the piece as a whole. Strive for a flow in the spacing. Avoid jerkiness.

I am taking in a lot at one time now, but the meaning of it will come to you once you begin to think in these terms. As soon as you break away from certain common limitations, one discovery leads to another. The size and taper of a dovetail has its meaning not just as "hardwood joint" or "softwood joint," but

also as a joint in a *particular* wood where color and texture play their part, and these are in turn part of the piece with its character: it may be angular, soft-curved, refined, robust, heavy. What I mean is *sensing* that the taper of each and every dovetail should not be so exact as to take the life out of it; we can determine an angle which we feel suits the wood and the purpose. Then, marking this, we can allow ourselves to be good, human craftsmen. Not sloppy, but just free enough to keep the work alive. In time we find ourselves marking the angles by eye rather than with a gauge. You would be surprised how accurate one can be without becoming rigid—it's a balance we arrive at, you see, a feeling. Useful—and satisfying.

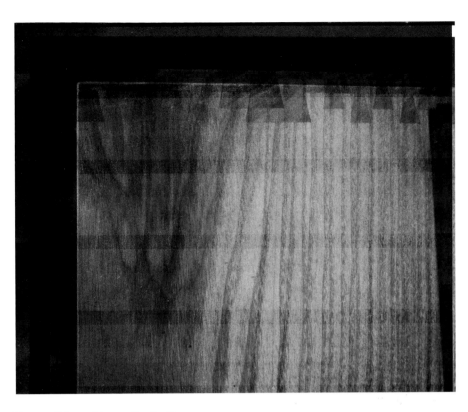

Dovetail in cabinet of ash. Note spacing.

Top side of cabinet: dovetails with edge of piece beveled to achieve a desired shading or "play" for the eye.

Dovetails. Cabinet in oak and ash. Since the case itself extends inside (beyond) leg at right, the pattern as a whole is balanced, the dovetails becoming successively smaller and closer spaced.

As we overcome one obstacle, find a way to do a certain part of our work more easily and better, it is a natural wish to want to perfect another part of it as well. We may begin by scribing all the way across our pieces—including where the dovetails will be, and also the spaces between the recesses; we do this at first, and find after a time how a scribe mark goes deeper than we imagined: it takes unnecessary planing to get past it. As our joints improve we want them at their best: we are even more irritated by those cross-grain lines. And because we have a guide block, we can scribe less deep, and only where we will be cutting the wood away. On the dovetails we mark between these: on the part with recesses, mark for each opening including the outer ones—and then on the outer edges themselves. A minimum of scribing, finally, instead of the usual chisel-starting, hard-to-remove marks. Saving effort need not be at the expense of quality, or the wholeness of our work: it can, in fact, add to both. Something similar occurs when we begin to realize that there's a difference between a dovetail that is lax, or droopy—and one with what I call flair. When we saw and chisel joints and then fit them directly as they are, we often find the resulting pattern a trifle rounded, I mean the dovetails are not as sharp and clear as we expected them to be. A corner not perfectly clean, a bruise made in the recess when cutting back, the fact that it is difficult to get an absolutely tight fit at the start of each saw-cut—all these details together leave the joint with something lacking. Again, I can only describe it as a lack of tension, or grace, or flair—use your own word. You will find the word and the meaning when you begin to pare the tapered dovetails before sawing the recesses for them. Take a fairly wide, absolutely sharp chisel and with it pare each dovetail carefully. First clean and at right angles to the end: then, as an extra touch, hollow them ever so slightly. Hold the piece way out where you are working and the chisel almost at the tip—tight—and practice making thin, sure cuts until you can pare a hardly visible hollow along both sides of each dovetail. On softwood this will of itself tend to be more, on very hard wood it will be almost too subtle to notice. But it will be there. To make sure the crispness isn't lost in a corner where you have sawn or chiseled not quite all the way, check each and every opening and, if need be, clean the corners with a fine pointed small knife. Or with a chisel you have reground to a double bevel; you will see now how easily one can slip it into an opening for a nicely proportioned dovetail. Then as the two parts of the joint are pressed together they will tend to be very tight at the corners and the outside of each dovetail—instead of being less perfect just there, as is often the case. Each dovetail will have a tension now, a clarity of its own.

Earlier I said dovetails should have flair. Maybe flair is something that has to be definite and noticeable, I don't know. The sharpness of line we have now is not so much an actual outward sweep of the bevels as it is a tension.

Not enough to fuss over? The main thing is that the joint is

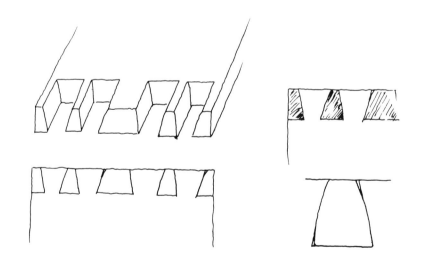

Dovetails as they tend to be: a bit lax, or limp, with small faults at the corners and the outside edge where the cuts were started.

Paring dovetails: those at right are slightly scooped (pared); at left is dovetail with surfaces as sawn (before paring).

Use a very sharp chisel and a firm grip.

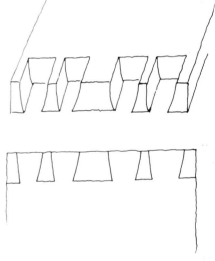

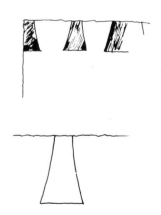

Dovetails neatly pared and carefully fitted have tension and clarity.

155

tight? Perhaps. And yet, what is it that causes us to experience some things more vividly or intensely than others? Granted, not everyone will notice these details, this care. But if the piece as a whole is good someone will surely like it. And a part of their liking will be details so natural as to pass, unnoticed, into the pleasure of experiencing the piece.

While on the subject of dovetails, let me talk a little about drawers as well. In the accompanying series of photos I have tried to include most of the basic steps without being too kindergartenish.

The first principle of a good drawer is that it fit. The difference between a good drawer and just a drawer is that one fits well and the other fits poorly. Besides these simple truths we have a number of other facts to keep in mind: drawers should be well put together. They can be more or less decorative as you choose, but they should work smoothly at all times of the year.

If there is a secret of well-fit drawers, it is one we easily recognize by now—that of method, patience, and consistency. To make a drawer that fits nicely is a bit more than just making a box. When we have a fine drawer that is at home in a piece just as fine, then we have done a good job, and can be proud.

Having started my cabinetmaking in Europe, before the popularity of drawers with runners, I may seem a little old-fashioned. To me the best drawers are those without runners, drawers fit properly into a space

where they float, so to speak, with an easy and even action. The best of them have a special quality; not only are they beautifully made throughout, but the action is easy in and almost all the way out. Then, just before the drawer would leave the piece where it belongs, it stiffens a trifle: instead of becoming loose, wobbling, and then letting go, it needs coaxing before you can pull it out completely. This action has to be experienced in order to be fully appreciated.

I hear someone say we can get a better action with runners—especially on the larger types of drawer. That's true—just as it is true that whatever aspect of our craft we approach this way, there will be an efficient, easier-to-do counterpart for those who lean in another direction. My own conviction is that we must pay a price for the element of engineering which creeps in with some slick solutions; for me, the price is too high. I've seen some craftsmen give way to the temptation of hidden runners routed into drawer-sides: the next step just might be routed joints, drawers put together with metal pins, plywood bottoms—a whole landslide of steps made easier. You understand, it's the attitude I am worried about, not the lack of skill. One can have fairly large, beautifully done drawers on runners, which may come through in front and become interesting handles or pulls high up or along the middle of the drawer side. The whole solution nicely balanced, joints, runners, dimensions, everything in a logical and pleasing harmony. And all

of it with a sensitive touch, rounded edges, pattern of dovetails, shape of handles all personally done. That would convince me. That would prove the craftsman is more than clever. As things are, drawers are an often-neglected part of cabinetmaking—inconsistent with the tone and aspirations of the rest of the piece. Good action, yes. But without the feeling of sensitivity that should be a part of it.

As I said, a fine drawer requires a perfect fit. To achieve such a fit with the minimum of grief, keep all your measurements exact and your tolerances as small as possible. And here make a note: the fit begins with the space that will take the drawer. So from the start, concentrate on this space: it, too, has its fine points. The sides must be clean, and true, the top and bottom—whether the surfaces of a cabinet, or separate frames, must be flat. Now one more thing: this evenly squared opening should be just a *fraction of a fraction* wider at the back than up front. This difference of width is difficult to measure, so don't measure it. Take a piece of plywood or Masonite, cut it to an even, snug fit with the front: it should gradually "let go" as you slide it back. Not wobble loosely but just move, smooth and free, as will the drawer—if we do this right. The height of our space can likewise increase at the back—though this is much less important than that the width do so: at any rate. See that the height does not *decrease* back there.

156

Drawers with unconventional "runners" resulting in nicely shaped pulls or grips. Fantasy and patience will lead to still other, and better, solutions.

I won't go into the various ways of assuring that the space or pocket has this "let go" margin, but it stands to reason one must relate it to the rest of the piece and how we plan things. In a cabinet we are often dependent on the sides for drawer space—consequently the top and bottom pieces with their joints should result in the sides being where we want them—and our inside space exact too. Keep this in mind, and plan accordingly. Don't trust measurements! Put the cabinet, etc. together dry, and then check these front-back tolerances. If the piece is doweled, and of solid wood, you can plane a little on the inside surfaces to correct things. But with dovetail joints, remember not to let the top and bottom pieces narrow towards the back!

As a rule I have drawers that are less than the width of the cabinet, with a partition between: I can then taper this partition so as to get the desired width of both spaces. It is usual to fit such partitions as sliding dovetails, or tongues: I tried this, but found the fits entirely dependent upon the sides (or other bordering surfaces) being improbably exact. Now I fit these partitions butted flush into the space, plane them exactly right—and then insert a spline into each end of the partition; the thickness of the spline in turn corresponds to small, neat grooves routed in the cabinet sides. This method is simpler than it sounds. And, I think, safer than almost any other when we are striving for that perfect fit.

Back of cabinet before gluing. Rabbet for back (frame and panel) has small margin left at corner, to be trimmed later (after gluing).

Routing groove in cabinet side for partition with spline. Note heel or stop on plywood guide.

As to the drawers themselves: these are, to put it simply, boxes made to exact measurements; 1/64 inch here is the difference between a good and a bad fit. I use measuring sticks on which I mark with notches the exact width, height and depth of each drawer and supply these with arrows, *w,h,d.* How much to allow? Let's take the most important measurement—the width, which must be an absolutely perfect fit. A common error here is to allow too much, 1/16 inch or more. "Better too big than too small." Not necessarily better; many errors are made planing down to size—a side out of line, the front or back suddenly too small; this happens all too easily, especially since such fitting makes us eager. On the width of an ordinary drawer made of fairly hard wood (ash, mahogany, maple), allow a total of about 1/32 inch on the width of the front and back pieces. Then when you scribe—and this is all-important—arrange it so as to bring the side pieces only a hair inside the pin-ends of the front and back. The usual mistake is to let these tolerances get out of hand, thinking perhaps of the dovetail ends which are not quite sharply sawn, and expecting to "plane everything right later." Avoid this. Keep the joints crisp and clean, the surfaces of drawer parts smooth and true—and *use the smallest possible margins* when fitting. In time you will approach the ideal: a drawer put together so that you will only need to file the dovetail ends a trifle, take a few light strokes with a polishing plane along each side, true the top and bottom edges less than 1/32 inch—coax the drawer into the opening, perhaps touch it here and there with a plane set to a less than paper-thin cut—and then slide the finished drawer into place. Try this, please. Practice coming very close in your measurements, working neatly, having your tools perfectly tuned, your bench clean and the vise true. Clamp any part or drawer so as to be able to work safely—and plane it to fit, don't scrape and sand and sweat. Plane light and smooth—learn to sense when a surface is flat, a corner true, a measurement right on. It's a satisfying feeling. And the sides of a drawer (or cabinet) with their dovetail patterns can never be quite as appealing, as clear and fresh and in focus as when they have been skillfully planed and left that way for us to enjoy.

Fitting partitions before making grooves and splines.

Filing dovetail-ends on brittle wood: tape on file prevents scratching of drawer sides while filing the protrusions.

Plane set very fine for final fitting of drawer.

The height of a drawer is not constant; being of solid wood, it varies with the degree of moisture in the air, which in turn relates to the time of year. On a height of four inches the come and go—even in pine—won't exceed 1/16 inch; with stable hardwoods this should stay under 1/32 inch. When taking out stock, there is no point in having the front and side pieces higher than just beyond a tight fit: otherwise you will not only have too much planing to do—with resulting errors—but will also tend to misjudge the placement of the outer dovetails and later have to plane these thinner than you intended. After all: with the rest of the joint just as you wanted it, it is embarrassing to be left with an outer dovetail out of tune.

The back piece of a fine drawer is as a rule fitted down about 1/4 inch from the top; the reason being that a drawer often runs under a surface (cabinet top, frame, between two horizontal partitions, etc.)—and as the drawer comes forward its back is pressed upward. With the back piece flush with the side, you get a scraping and binding there. Let the back piece down a little. And remember: it has to come up, too, enough for the bottom with its nicely rounded lip to slide into the small groove you will rout in the sides and front piece. You want that groove, and the underside of the drawer bottom, up a bit from the lower edge of each side. Thus, on a drawer say four inches high, the bottom will be about 3/16 inch thick, the distance you lessen the back piece should be somewhere near 1/4 inch both up and down.

Laying out: back of drawer with scribe mark (right) for groove which will take bottom.

Front of same drawer is same width (height) as side pieces.

Laying out back piece, side, and bottom in relation to later fit. Bottom is shown here without lip. The side piece will have a groove to take this lip when it is made. The scribe mark designates the top of the groove and allows for the thickness of the bottom plus clearance for the drawer to slide free.

That groove for the bottom is a matter of neatness and attention, too; remember to put your drawer together dry and plane the lower front corners flush. Also plane the margins at the back equal on both sides before you rout the groove. Set a scribe for that back margin, make a practice cut or two on an extra piece. You will want the drawer bottom to have a little leeway up front; make the groove deeper there than in the side pieces.

Work cautiously, in relation to the result you desire, not time, or money, or someone else's opinion of what your work should be. Think! For instance: when a cabinet is of solid wood, its depth *varies*, whereas that of a drawer inside the cabinet remains *constant*: allow for this when laying out! A drawer that is too deep is like a lottery ticket with a losing number.

The front of the drawer is trimmed flush at the corners before routing the groove for the solid wood bottom.

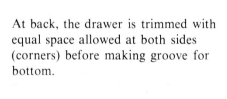

At back, the drawer is trimmed with equal space allowed at both sides (corners) before making groove for bottom.

164

Routing the groove for the drawer bottom. A piece of plexiglass (for small work) lessens the opening in the router table. The mark on the guide corresponds to the position of the router bit.

Just as you must have the parts of a drawer correct in order to make a groove for the bottom, so too the back of a cabinet needs to be exactly flush all round before you can cut a neat rabbet for the back piece. Form the habit of trimming the corners and having all the edges straight the first time you put the piece together (dry): do not force together and take apart something every other minute to check just one detail each time. It may be a help to make little memos at various stages of the work such as laying out, after the case is first assembled, before fitting various details, gluing and so on. I do this on a scrap of paper or a chip—and it helps, especially when there are interruptions. Keep in mind, too, that in cabinet cases, boxes, and drawers, the outside dovetails should be planned in relation to what's going to happen in that particular corner (or part): if you are going to cut a rabbet, make the dovetail there large enough to take the rabbet without being weakened; on a drawer you may need to get past (above) the lowest dovetail with the groove for the bottom piece. These are merely pointers now, you will discover their meaning in relation to your own kind of work as you go along.

Drawer with groove in sides and front, and bottom piece shaped to fit.

Likewise at the front corners, you need to consider how the door or doors will swing, where the hinges will fit. Is the action such as to allow a drawer to pass the door when it is open? Do you want a lock or wooden catches for the doors? These and other simple things, if you think clearly and are interested, become filled with possibilities. A door is not just something we set up against the front of a cabinet case or bureau and then plane flush with the sides; there are so many other and more fanciful ways of doing the same basic thing. We can pull the door in a bit at each side, making shadings there, or set the door in a nicely rounded rabbet to give a thinner and more refined appearance. We can—well, you will find out for yourself. What I mean here is that logic, thinking everything through *caring about those little details*, is part of a final difference in our work.

We can't avoid the trial of gluing our dovetails—though at times we'd like to. Glue we must, so we might as well do it right. When you are making something that is involved, and promising, and are almost to the point of gluing—a red warning light should go on some place. Have you smoothed the insides of the piece? Rounded the edges softly, treated the inside surfaces with polish or wax? Pared the edges at a corner where the parts protrude so as to avoid chipping these later? And even when you have done all this—are you sure the parts will go together at the joints: all the way, that is,

tight—without your having to whack with a hammer, rush for clamps, sweat and strain almost as much as the piece of wood you are manhandling? There is no reason to avoid tapping the parts of a joint together dry to assure their going home later on: the joint will not suffer, or become less tight by this—not if it is a good fit, it won't. But of course, if the fit is imperfect, and you force it, hammer hard to get it there (leaving bruises) and then work it loose by wiggling it back and forth—the joint will suffer, and those who don't know better will say they told you so.

Try your joints before gluing. Carefully, using a block to tap against. If the wood is hard and brittle and has no give, be doubly cautious. *Any joint that does not fit fairly easily when dry will not do so with the help of glue:* the whole thing may jam, and stick when only partly tight. Pare a bit more, be patient, keep working until the joint responds, and you can get the parts together tightly without violence. Even with softer woods you should do this at least once, to make sure you will be able to do it again, also to check the roundings and the groove for the bottom. If you work well enough, you will be able to predetermine the outside width before gluing; not to micrometric tolerances, but close enough to assure yourself that the drawer is not too narrow.

I use blocks made "soft" with a layer of 1/16 inch cardboard glued to one side for tapping home joints. And a piece of

cardboard on the work bench, so the dovetail tips on the down side of the piece have somewhere to go, and allow the side in all the way. When gluing larger, more complicated joints I have "soft" blocks the length of each joint and a clamp or two handy. No, I do not clamp my work together. If worst comes to worst (and it just might), I put a block along each joint and clamp tight for a moment only, move the clamp farther along the joint, tighten—and then lay the clamp or clamps aside. But I assure you: most of the time I do not have to clamp at all. Nor bang violently. The way some people glue a piece together looks like a wrestling match. Wham, bang, tools all over the place, clamps this way and that, cabinet or drawer sides bowed like springboards, glue oozing along edges and in corners. How do you know when you have right angles when hardly a line is straight under all that strain? Use diagonals. Why is excess glue so difficult to wipe clean? Instead of having to wipe away—use less of it. Any glue pushed out should not have been there in the first place.

To glue properly, you must first be ready to glue. The pieces neat, as nearly completed as possible, all properly marked (with pyramids), placed logically on the bench; glue, hammer, blocks, a small brush or thin piece of wood as an applicator, diagonal sticks, a square if you so wish—as well you might when the work is small. With all this and a clear head you'll get by unaided.

A FEW OTHER JOINTS

Once more, for the sake of the record, I do not exclude or even minimize the help machines can be to us.

This help includes the making of certain joints which, though done with the efficient accuracy of our machines, can still be given a personal touch: to the exactness of the machine we add the spice of playfulness.

Shown here are a few such joints. They are made largely with what might be called a production method: the table saw and horizontal mortiser are set up to do precisely what we want them to do, on one joint—or ten.

At first glance a production sort of thing, yes. Though the difference between this and what a factory might do is apparent, if we look closely, and feel: the tenons protrude slightly, are wedged, and made pleasantly soft to both eye and touch. Such details can be done by industry, but I doubt if they will or should be, since a part of their appeal goes with something other than a mass-produced product. Besides, the cost would be prohibitive.

Through-joints with a personal touch.

Why not do them entirely by hand, then? The answer is in the result: if you can do them well enough by hand, more power to you! But well enough should be good; and not just once or twice, either. Certainly, having tried, you are bound to know more about your saws and chisels.

For now, let's try it with the help of machines. Have the blade of your table saw sharp and clean. I use oven cleaner on mine; remove the blade, put it on a piece of paper or a plastic bag, spray with oven cleaner, let set for a few minutes, rub with an old toothbrush, then rinse and wipe dry. If the blade is sharp, it is now as good as new.

My horizontal mortiser is part of the simple table-saw I have, and has no feed attachment. Even if I could afford it, I would not buy such an accessory because it takes more than it gives: by the time you get it set up, you could have done the work just feeding it by hand. The feed attachment is for doing multiples. One uses very fast cutting bits then; holding and feeding by hand with these bits is, if not dangerous, at least a very tense kind of work: you feel the piece is apt to get away from you—which makes things even worse.

Try bottoming end-mill bits such as the one shown. Yes, they are for metal, and they do cut slowly. But, oh, so cleanly! Without rattling or grabbing. It's just that you have to be a little patient—which isn't asking too much, really when you have seen the results. These router bits are available in many different sizes, three- or four-fluted. They last a long, long time.

Choose one, make a trial mortise, and then saw all your tenons—full width—to a thickness fit. From here on, plan carefully. Decide how you want the joints; which part should be resawn into a tenon or tenons that will pass through another tenon, or maybe overlap it. You can lay these out to be decorative but also proper; the ones at the top of a leg, for instance, will have a heel on the inside for added strength, since you want the tenon itself down as far as it will go. Saw them neat and clean. Before you work them further, mark for the corresponding mortises. Now round the edges of the tenons as needed: I do this by first paring at the base with a fine knife, then taking a few cautious cuts out towards the end (watch the grain!) and finally finishing off with a file to an exact half-round. Exact, or it won't look good.

Then I make the mortises. Where one passes through another, insert a filler-piece to avoid chipping when you use the mortiser, or, as with the squared ones, a drill and then a chisel. Fit one tenon tight, mark it for whatever cutting needs to be done, remove it, shape it as marked; now all you have to do is to touch it up after it is glued in place, before you fit and glue the other part. (It only sounds complicated. And it applies only to joints that "bite into" each other).

We now have what may seem like parts of a Chinese puzzle. And like those in a puzzle, they need to be put together right. And glued, and wedged that way.

Saw for the wedges. I start my cuts just past the half-rounds of each tenon, and slant them a trifle inward so as not to weaken the tenon. On a square tenon it is nice to make a diagonal cut. Do not make the cut too thin! It can close like a clamshell when you are gluing, and the wedge won't start, or will start and then break. Have the wedges exactly the width of your tenons, with a long taper so they will go far in.

Fit the joint dry now: it can be done without accident if you just take things slow and easy. Tap it in or out, don't wiggle or twist it. Use a block so as not to bruise the parts. But before you take a joint apart for gluing, check that the wedges fit, mark where the round (or bevel) on each tenon will end, and think of how you want to shape it. Do this shaping carefully; *complete it before gluing!* Later will be too late. It is a small detail, but important—that's what our joint is about.

In your mind now go through the entire process of gluing, including the clamps, and make the special pressure blocks you'll need at the outside of each joint. These blocks should have grooves *a little larger* than the protruding part of each tenon. Since I work alone, I tack crosspieces on some of the blocks—cleats to hold them in place until I can get the clamp or clamps on.

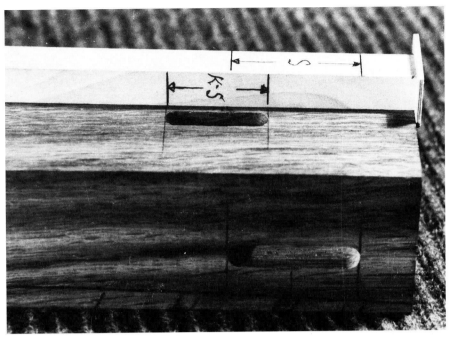

Bottoming end-mill cuts mortises cleanly.

Jig for exact placement of mortises. The lower mortise has been left partly finished to show the cleanness of the cut made with an end-mill bit.

Gluing through-joints: note the pressure block with groove to take the protruding end of the tenon, and the heel on the block to hold it in place until clamped.

I have heard someone say that getting the right pressure in the right place is half of gluing. Here it's more than half; since the ends of our tenons protrude, and there are the wedges to place. Unless we get everything right, there is no use attempting this sort of joint.

Do, dry run-through the gluing. Set up everything you need, notice whether you can get the clamps properly on the blocks—maybe these need to be taped in place. Have a few extra wedges handy, a small mallet, a saw (we cut off the end of each wedge rather than break it).

When you glue, use a very thin chip to get into the wedge-cuts, apply glue *sparingly and very neatly*—don't rush into this. Put full pressure on for just a moment to bring the parts home, quickly remove the clamp, tap the wedges in *straight*, saw flush with the tenon—clamp again if need be, and let dry. Later, file the wedge ends smooth.

I say nothing about wiping off excess glue on the outside. This is because I hope you won't have to. The reward of extreme neatness here is, I feel, worth the effort. These are simple, honest joints; there is nothing pretentious or awkward about them. They are very strong, and can be made finely dimensioned to suit a piece that is both elegant and interestingly put together.

Cabinet with ash case and stand of Swedish oak.

170

Views of the ash-oak cabinet showing
various joints.

FRAME-AND-PANEL WORK

It is generally easier for us to accept the care and labor involved in frame-and-panel doors or in the lid of a box done that way—than to regard a frame-and-panel back piece in a nice cabinet or bureau as a natural thing. In a showcase, yes, there it *shows*. But in just a cabinet, or other piece of furniture where the back is not so obvious—we hesitate.

Partly this is because of a misconception: we imagine this type of back entails more work than it really does. And then there is this attitude: after all, it is the back.

Try turning the argument around. Ask yourself: How fine a piece am I making, what sort of person am I hoping will want it? Will he or she notice the difference—and care? And finally: do I care? The answer should be yes. So be consistent. Do nice work all the way; front, back, bottom, and sides. Everything on a level which feels right. It's as simple as that: one who has pride wants to keep it.

Frames and panels are not really difficult to make. Once we get the basic idea and the hang of it, the work is pleasant, and rewarding—certainly more so than messing around with plywood and the like, spoiling tools while producing an indifferent result.

With our panel back we can use the same solid wood as in the rest of the piece, choosing interesting patterns, a darker or lighter shade for the panel itself, with the frame as a neat border between it and the case. Doing showcases in particular it is important to select the wood with fantasy and care. Try having the

panel of a lighter shade than the rest of the piece: you can create the feeling of light coming from somewhere inside the space.

Granted that in a jewelry box or a small cabinet about ten inches wide, a one-piece lid bottom or back of solid wood can be used, provided it is not glued in. But beyond that width a set-in

Frames-and-panel back in cabinet of English brown oak. Done with care, it shows attention to and use of sensitive qualities in the wood.

piece "floats" a good deal: a frame and panel becomes a more logical, and often more decorative, solution.

Do not make it heavy and awkward; keep the thicknesses down and the frame pieces fairly narrow. On a frame two feet high these can be 1 1/2 inches or 1 3/4 inches wide at most. For such a frame a thickness of 3/8 or 7/16 inch should do; on a two-by-three-foot frame it can be increased to about 1/2 inch, and the width to nearly two inches. These are merely suggestions. Remember, however: any thickness added to the frame is space taken from the cabinet itself. If it is a smallish cabinet or box, this does matter.

Usually I use a light strip of wood as a measuring stick for the outer dimensions of the frame. Add a fraction to the actual sizes of the rabbet in the cabinet case. Mark clearly "l" and "w" a sharp cross-line or a notch for each measurement. With this stick you needn't have numbers bouncing in your head all the while. This is a relief: there is enough concentrating to do already.

It is reassuring to have one or two extra pieces for the frame, just in case, and shorter, unusable cut-offs as a help in setting the saw when doing the joints. Work carefully. *Do not saw so as to have the ends (or is it edges?) of the joints protruding—especially those parts parallel to the visible line at the frame corners, since you want full pressure there when gluing.* A word more about these simple joints: Make the tenons (or fingers) *slightly more* than one third of the frame thickness, otherwise this part will be weaker than the other two together. Take your time with the saw especially; it is a treacherous machine. Clean the saw-blade before using. This work is a succession of steps properly done. The frame, to be enjoyed, must be neat.

Frame joint-sawn so as to ensure pressure and a tight fit (see text).

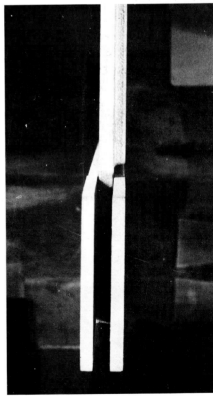

Thickness of panel in relation to the frame.

Cut the groove for the panel with a router or shaper, using a slot cutter with a small radius. This is because a large-radius cut such as a circular saw usually produces will run far out on the tenon part of the frame, weakening the joints.

Be sure the ends of the grooves are squared off so as to allow for the corners of the panel. Put the frame together dry, round all the inside edges neatly and evenly: you won't be able to get at these properly later, so do them now.

The panel should be two-thirds the thickness of the frame or a bit less: the strength of the back when finished lies in the frame itself, and not in the panel.

One important point here: we want the front (inside) surface of the panel to be just under that of the frame. This will make it easier to clamp and glue the frame and then later smooth and finish it at the corners. A panel with its fine surface above the level of the frame can be a real problem. Choose the wood sensibly, straight or intentionally tense, balanced lines in the frame, a nice shade and patterns for the panel. Think of how you will work those panel surfaces, remember that when you book-match certain woods you get not only changes in shades but also grain that goes different ways: this probably means you will have to work the final surface with a cabinetscraper or extra-fine plane. So when you edge-glue the pieces do it very carefully. You are saving work by taking care. Even small differences in thickness can throw you off when doing this kind of work.

Routing grooves in a frame. These are from ¼ to ⅜ inch deep.

The panel is just below the level of the frames to enable finishing joints at the corners after gluing without damaging the panel itself.

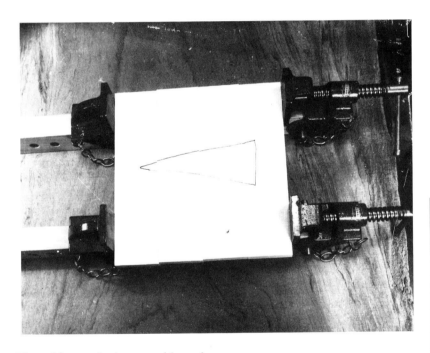

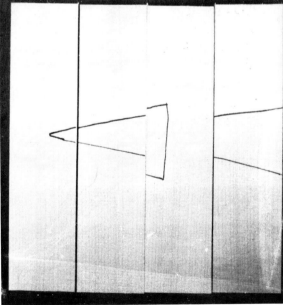

The cabinetmaker's pyramid mark again. When you make and glue panels, drawer bottoms, etc., this way of marking is a great convenience—and really infallible if used properly. Marking several surfaces to be glued, pyramids with double lines or with a vertical line through the pyramid can be used to identify various units.

On a measuring stick mark *exactly* the sizes for the panel: these are distances inside the grooves—*not just to the edges of the frame!* Check this: it is heartbreaking to cut a panel a mere 3/8 inch too short. Turning to the panel: we see that it is evenly thick, and that the *back* side does not need further surfacing down. We can finish the front after we make the lip to fit the groove (slot): just now it is more important to have an even thickness, as *any unevenness here transposes itself to the lip, which then becomes a poor fit.* Use a cutter with rounded tips (I regrind some of my regular ones) and machine a neat, even lip with a gentle changeover from flat to vertical. This, together with other soft edges and corners, gives the back piece much of its appeal. The lip is to fit snugly into the groove, but not jam there: The panel is a "live" piece of wood that will react to the seasons, expanding in summer and contracting in winter.

Now: will the panel as you have it fit, and float? Check this by clamping it and the frame together dry and tight. Think again about the margin you have allowed at the sides. Working during a warm and humid summer you know the wood is near its natural maximum—your panel will probably never be more than a negligible bit wider than it is now. But in mid-winter, when the air is cold and dry, the same panel will have shrunk; a hardwood one fifteen inches in width might move in almost 1/8 inch on each side. Allow for shrinkage when you do the fitting

in summertime, and for expansion when you fit it in winter.

The margins I have mentioned are presupposing your wood is dry, that is to say, it is stable in

the conditions of your workshop. I always work by stages: resaw wood I know is stable, let it settle nonetheless, glue together needed widths, let these

Routing lip in panel to fit groove made in all four parts of the frame.

The panel has a softly shaped lip with its corners neatly rounded.

Various details of a typical frame-and-panel construction.

Detail of back glued and finished, before it is fitted to the cabinet.

settle, too. I am the worrying kind: maybe that's why I have not had any bad disappointments with my frames and panels.

After you have checked the fit of your panel, and perhaps planed a little off each lip, or even redone an edge with its lip, smooth the surfaces, round the corners neatly, and apply a satiny finish to the panel as well as the inside edges of the frame.

Please don't use lacquer. As I have said earlier, you do not want people to wrinkle their nose when they open your cabinet. Oil, too is unsuitable, since it turns rancid when in an enclosed space. Use wax if you wish. Though polish made from shellac diluted to the consistency of water is even better. Apply it a little at a time, evenly; let it dry for fifteen minutes or so between coats, sand lightly, and then repeat. Three or four coats will give a nice satiny surface. With the rest of the cabinet treated the same way inside, it will remain sweet-smelling and pleasant for many years.

Now, when you glue the back piece together, be careful. Clamp it dry once more, with cross-pieces between the cabinet clamps so as to raise the piece about an inch and allow for the handclamps and blocks at the four joints. I usually make these blocks of 3/8- or 1/2-inch wood and then glue a piece of thin cardboard on one side of each to keep the block from sticking to the frame. Set everything up: glue, rags, clamps, pressure blocks (*two* for each corner), a square, etc. See that you have made pyramid marks on the extreme outside edges of the frame, facing front. Don't turn the parts wrongly when putting on glue! Use glue sparingly; avoid letting it run into the panel-grooves. *Remember to slide the panel in before it is too late. Have it facing the right way* (this sounds silly on paper, but makes sense when you are alone doing the work). Knock the frame into square by hand, wipe clean, and then clamp. Check the squareness.

Later, smooth off the corners flush and put a finish on the rest of the frame. You will see now why it is good to have the panel surface set back a little.

When you fit the back to your cabinet, do it with the same care you have used hitherto, cleaning it square on two consecutive sides first, fitting these to the rabbet in the cabinet—then bit by bit planing in the other two sides. The rabbet, by the way, should be just a trifle deeper than the thickness of the frame: you can file the edges a touch to avoid the harsh, irritating lines of fits that are nearly but not quite flush.

It is usual to glue the back piece into the cabinet. Do this cautiously, with as little glue as possible, the cabinet case and frame protected by pressure blocks or strips of wood whereever you use clamps. On some occasions, usually in a showcase, I have made a wider rabbet than needed for gluing and then fastened the back neatly with small screws. Since the back is such a vital part of a glassed-in piece, there is an advantage to being able to remove it in case of

a bad scratch or other accident.

I have dwelt largely upon the frame and panel in back pieces, no doubt because the use of this construction seems to be neglected. And even with the more common uses of it I think many of us are limiting ourselves. Whether the lid of a small box or a wardrobe door, a frame-and-panel solution is not merely some nice wood with a frame around it. Nor does it need to be flat, as is often the case. Or awkward in its dimensions, or indifferent in the way the wood has been chosen.

Nicely paired doors, a single door, or even a small lid done as a frame and panel can set the mood for the rest of the piece. In fact it sometimes should do so, since it is not merely a technically sound solution, but also a prominent part of the piece as a whole.

A frame can be rectangular or even square, just straight lines to start with: yet by the way we use the rhythm of the wood—its grain and shadings—we can give our frame a definite character. It can be made to convey the feeling of mild curves, almost an oval friendly to the eye. Or of an outward, sharp-cornered shape. We can slant the wood pattern of two doors towards their common middle, and create the sense not of flatness, but of the doors being set in a slight V: when they actually are so angled we can accentuate that V form if we wish. Our doors or lids need not be flat surfaces: we can use a frame-and-panel solution for convex or concave forms—again choosing the wood so as to work with the

shapes, not only of the door but of the piece as it will be experienced later on. When you try to envision a piece and predict its appearance, think of its proper use, and how someone else—who likes it and will be living with it—will be most apt to see it from day to day.

I began by sawing the frames for curved doors out of thick stock. This works well with fairly narrow doors, such as those in pairs, though this way it is somewhat difficult to predict the final grain pattern of parts meant to be properly matched. Making wider doors, I laminate the curved frames. One-piece or laminate, such shapes involve some exact planing and consistent accuracy: all of it has to be done right. Which means being awake—and patient.

Earlier I mentioned the practical advantage of keeping the panel itself a trifle under the surface of the frame, almost flush This applies mostly to back pieces, since these with their frames are essentially one decorative surface. When we are sure of ourselves and can work carefully enough, it is interesting to experiment with panels that swell in soft relief, like cushions with finely worked corners, or those set farther back from the face of the frame so as to give a feeling of depth. The shadings around the panel edges, the way the lip is shaped into the panel surface, how we round the edges of the frame—all these details contribute to make this work more rewarding to do and more pleasing to see. On a curved door, *shape your panel to the frame rather than trying to bend it into place.* The work of planing a panel to a desired curve is very satisfying. So is harmonizing the patterns of the frame with the curve itself: especially when we work not so much with coarse obvious grain and lines—as with wood that responds to a subtle touch.

It is safer not to risk your whole door by fitting the panel "for keeps" to grooves in the frame and then assembling the frame around it as with a back piece. A rabbet made to take the panel at the desired depth is better here: you finish this off with nicely beveled strips on the inside, the panel is secured—but can be removed if need be. This method is more relaxing to follow, since you'll be able to fit, glue, and finish the frame door without worrying about the panel itself.

I do believe there is interesting work yet to be done with frame-and-panel construction. Like some other traditional aspects of our craft this technique has been too much taken for granted, and as a result is neglected; or used without joy or fantasy. It is so with some sides of the cabinet-maker's work: we are aware only of their general uses and significance. But it is when we move beyond these rigid solutions, to our own discoveries and sense of confidence that the interesting part really begins.

From care and patience the step is not far to luck. The main thing is to feel all along that this work is not unimportant, but a consistent part of how we want the whole piece.

Cabinet with frame-and-panel doors. The frame is padouk; the panels, natural pearwood. About twenty by thirty-two inches.

LATCHES, HINGES, AND FITTINGS

As far back as I can remember I've been carving or whittling wood. So perhaps it is natural that from the time I started as a cabinetmaker, my pieces have always contained details which are done with fine knives and other small tools.

Knives are a neglected chapter in the cabinetmaker's tale. Most of the knives available are awkward. The Swedish *slöjd* knives are certainly worse than their reputation: *slöjd* means handcraft, and I suppose these knives served the purpose of cutting (not really carving) certain rather simple handcraft objects. Even the smaller so-called carving knives are ungraceful; the tips of the ones we are apt to use most are too wide, the edge we'd normally press with a thumb doing certain cuts is rough-ground and has an irritating feel. And at the risk of sounding hypercritical, I will say this: the handles of most carving knives do not feel as though they were made for someone who does a lot of carving and does it nicely.

When it comes to doing small, neat details, most of us cut *towards: we pull the knife into the cut,* rather than pushing it as one does with coarser work. We *carve* delicate things, we don't whittle them in the ordinary sense. Consequently, instead of a handle that tapers at its far (butt) end, we like one that swells nicely and ends in a shape which serves as a stop, and rather than have a neutral round or oval shape, we want the handle to curve with the

Knives. At right is *slöjd* type all too commonly used. The knife at left is more suitable for delicate work.

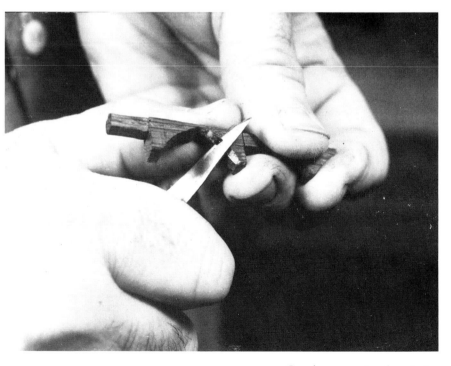

Carving consoles for shelves.

180

natural way we hold it as we do this cutting *towards*. A good handle is simply a shape which feels right when we are working well.

As to the knife-tip: we use the last inch of our knife a great deal. It is not for poking holes or marking a line: we carve with that tip. Many of the sensitive shapes in a door-handle, latch, console, or the like are shapes with minute bevels, carvings whose radius can be cut neatly only with a knife-tip that is *narrow and razor-sharp*. We do this carving towards us, with our hand rather than our arm. It's an opening and closing of the hand movement: holding the knife far down and very tight we tense our fingers and forearm and make cuts that have a lot of power, but are controlled. We can stop at any time, twist the knife in a tight curve, or out of the cut altogether. And if we do want to push into a cut, we flip the knife the other way, hold the wood in our left hand, and with our left thumb on the back of the knife we press hard, and with a controlled tension steer the cut exactly as we wish. It's a nice, strong, scooping motion, all under control.

From this you will understand that unless we have the right knife—and use it properly, we will not be able to do the detailed work I am talking about.

When it comes to the way we solve problems involving the details and personal touches in our pieces—let's say a door and how it should open, whether or not it needs a handle—there are, I suppose, fundamentally two different approaches. Both begin with a logical function: but somewhere early they take divergent paths.

We have a cabinet door: we want a handle on it because as a rule a door opens with a handle, and (again as a rule) this is on the left side of the door—which we then swing to the right. With a pair of doors the right-hand one should be opened first—still towards our right. Now a handle is a grip, more or less decorative, but a grip. We can use a router to make half-round grooves in a fairly wide piece, cut a tenon along the opposite end, divide it lengthwise, shape the ends of the grooved piece on a belt sander—and there is our handle, or handles if we so wish. This is the shorter and more traveled path, the one we are most apt to be shown.

The other is a bit longer, and starts farther back. I have a cabinet with a door; as a whole it gives me a certain feeling. Sometimes the mood of the piece is so simple that I don't believe the door needs a handle. I'm not a conventional craftsman, and maybe for this reason some of my tools are unconventional: I am forever altering standard tools to suit my various whims. With these I can now imagine many ways the door might look and work very well without a handle. I'll keep that curved surface clean, those proportions uncluttered: the door will open nicely with a groove along its right side, a simple profile which will accentuate the edges of the door and feel good for the fingertips of a right hand. Why right hand? Well; walk over to the cabinet as it hangs on the wall, reach out searching for a way to open the door—probably you are right-handed—and since there is no handle, you'll find your fingertips groping along that right edge. So a shallow groove there feels natural, good, as does the motion of opening the door towards your left. A fancy handle might be tempting, a chance to show I can carve a little—but here, now, this groove is better.

I can spin my feelings further. Make a similar groove on the other side of the door: it becomes a means of balancing the shadings on the cabinet—and provides still another way to show the decorative rounded ends of the brass hinges; their shape blends suggestively into the groove there. Use your fantasy, but keep the balance of purpose and fun. Perhaps the door (or doors) together with a particular cabinet want handles; not just logically—one can have two doors and still no handles—but as a part of what I feel this cabinet should be. Now, because I have all sorts of fine knives, carving chisels, and small files, as well as a model maker's vise, I can allow myself to muse over a handle that I'll shape as I look at the cabinet. If the cabinet seems delicate, a bit ethereal as some are, I'm apt to carve a handle that is fairly long, thinning out and then ending in a flare which has a hollow for a thumb; someone will be encouraged to take this handle with just a thumb and forefinger-tip, and to open the door gently—after all, it is but a small door in a sensitive piece.

Handles for cabinet doors.

Another time the piece is more robust; the handle then becomes larger and of another shape, requiring a firmer hold, conveying another feeling. I do the tenons on all these handles with the help of my fine table saw and cut the first shape on the bandsaw. After that I have only the cabinet, the door, and my response to these as a guide. I carve the handle, fuss with placing it at various points on the door, make a guess—and then cut a very neat mortise—all the way through—using one of my four-fluted cutters and the horizontal mortiser. Later the handle with this tenon will be fitted and finally wedged.

In a drawer, everything will probably turn out differently. The height at which a drawer is placed can determine how we like to use it, whether a handle there should be horizontal or vertical or round, to be grasped in a certain way— or merely flipped forward with one finger-tip under a narrow, downward-curved tongue. Sometimes, when the drawer is close behind a door, I have a small opening in its front, carved finger-friendly. And because I like to do neat dovetails, I can depart from the conventional half-lapped ones, and, when I want to, let mine be open, visible from in front as a straight lined light-and-dark pattern that is an intentional part of the drawer in this particular surrounding. (I will not, in my freedom, allow the dovetail-ends to face forward—*that* would be wrong!)

Within reason, I have the freedom to do as I feel and choose to do, and know I can do well enough. This freedom is right, and a kind of richness. It keeps me from tiring.

For years I've been carving handles, wooden latches, consoles for shelves, and I still enjoy doing this. The tight upward curve of each console is one surface, not easy to cut cleanly time after time; then I must bevel it on each side, following its curve with a thin, easy cut that comes off in one curl; it has to be a single clean cut, leaving the shape burnished and clear to the curious eye. Holes in the cabinet I drill with the aid of a template on which I have determined the position of each shelf. I'm apt to arrange it so that a shelf can be moved one or two pegs up or down from where I myself would best like it. The holes up front

Consoles: the peg part being sawn to length.

are fairly close to the edge, the ones in back I place far enough from the back piece to allow reaching without scratching the frame or panel there: small considerations, these, but after they become habit it is good to use them.

A word about drilling those shelf-holes. Have a stop on your drill. Mark the end of the template which corresponds to "down" in the cabinet. Be sure you have the cabinet sides properly marked, too. Start the holes slowly and neatly; countersink them a little before you apply finish to the insides of the pieces. I usually have a piece of scrap with holes made with the same drill—when I carve the consoles, I fit them to this test piece.

My tools are tuned to all my whims. So are the few items of hardware I use. My hinges are very simple. The knife-type ones I have made by a small machine shop, according to my various needs. They are easy to fit neatly, and give me a wide choice in the way I fit and hang my doors—which in turn allows me more freedom in composing cabinets and the like. Once you start thinking about it, there are so many things one can do with a door or doors, when you have the means! These pin hinges are made of brass, with a turned steel pin. The lower ones have a thin bushing (washer) as part of the pin—which brings the door up a trifle to avoid scraping.

Consoles: trimming and fitting the peg to trial holes.

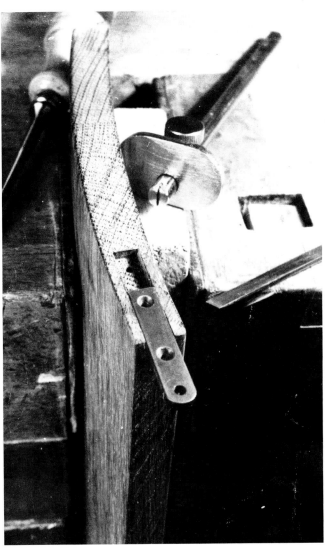

Fitting one half of a hinge to a curved door.

Some of the hinges I use. These are brass, with steel pins. The ones that fit into the bottom of the cabinet have a washer turned as part of the pin: this prevents the door from scraping.

If I want special small hinges or fittings of silver I'll have these made, too—hoping to make a jewelry box or similar piece nice enough for them. And for someone as well. We have very fine real cast brass butt hinges in Sweden; properly machined, either polished or dull finish. I like the latter best.

Students ask me about special fittings of wood, wrought iron, or brass, and how decorative these should be. What can I say?

To myself I remember something St.-Exupéry wrote, to the effect that a thing is at its best not when there is nothing more to add, but when there is nothing more to take away. Hardly a message for our times, I must sadly admit.

These details, like the rest of what we do, are a matter of taste. And taste means different things to different people. To me, wooden hinges on a table-leaf seem pretentious; besides, I feel

they are apt to break under certain probable conditions of use. But to someone else they are just tops, real craftsmanship. One person likes wrought-iron fittings on a small chest, another thinks they should be on a barn door. All around us are gaudy things, the overdone, the expensively cheap, distortions like a lamp on a classic Japanese theme—fitted with a plastic shade.

A lower door-hinge nicely fitted.

Well-made butt hinges. These are Swedish, of cast brass, satin finished.

Door-latches of hard wood (rosewood in this case) showing spring, and screw with which tension of latch can be adjusted "just right." These latches are at the top of a cabinet.

Yet why be negative here? Why regret the facts of showiness in a showy time? In the showiest place of all there's a lot of very interesting work being done: in America there are the energy and curiosity and conviction and confusion to do the best as well as the worst. A good deal of both, often alongside one another.

I feel vulnerable having to explain that small wooden latches tucked inside a cabinet are not a rustic effect, but only the result of my liking the sound of a door closing with a soft swishing of wood against wood instead of a metallic click. These latches are of very hard wood, usually in harmony with the piece itself, and they have a little spring in a hole underneath; the latch can be adjusted by turning the screw that holds it in place. The spring itself is from a ball-point pen, the half-and-half one made by BIC. I go to a bookstore and buy five or six of these pens; the lady hands them to me, and then one by one I break them open, throw the halves and the ink-tube in the wastebasket, stuff the springs in my pocket, and walk out.

187

Besides the latch holding the door at the top, there is a wooden "button," a length of dowel with its tip rounded, set in a countersunk hole in the bottom piece, that keeps the door from sagging.

I have never been inventive. The pivoting door opener (shown in the photos) for a cabinet with two doors and no handles works satisfactorily, but is hardly ingenious. Some of my students have improved on this and other ideas, and made all sorts of clever fittings that are modestly decorative and yet quite functional. Much remains to be done here; one can imagine many kinds of interesting and amusing solutions for drawers and doors that snap shut, or open at the touch of a finger, or won't open at all—until we find that well-hidden catch.

As for shelves in a cabinet, some might have the front edge straight, others I curve inward a bit—as a whim, or because it seems logical, since one can then more easily reach something on a lower shelf. These shelves are often beveled along the lower front edge, and the bevel is not even, but increases towards the middle of the shelf; I think this gives a feeling of upward tension, a kind of lift that keeps the shelf from seeming "tired." I try to choose the wood so the grain along that front edge works in a slight upward arc, too, and is part of the tension there.

Pivoting door opener set in the bottom of a cabinet with curved doors. With the doors wholly open or closed, the end of the opener itself is flush with the cabinet bottom.

Such small touches are perhaps easier to do if you expect a tangible reward for them (though then they are apt to be showy). But for some of us they are a part of being consistent in the way we feel about a certain piece—how it will be used, what mood it conveys, how usage and time will affect it and the people who like it enough to live with it.

A bookshelf of untreated, natural pearwood, and detail of drawer.

More often than not people notice these details. Let's hope this occurs after they have begun to like the piece: probably it is so, since the details are unobtrusive. Then I am happy. Once in a while, at an exhibition perhaps, some one has turned a shelf upside-down; its edge with that bevel wrong now, and for a while no one sees the difference.

In our attempts at sensitivity we are dependent upon the sensitivity of others. Perhaps we need to face this fact with a touch of humor. There was once a man who ran a school for cabinetmakers. He had the honorary title of "professor," and when I knew him he was already an old man. Strangely, he hadn't done much cabinetmaking himself, though he knew a good deal about it; he was famous as a designer of furniture. He was partial to decorative things, carved or with inlay or naively painted, many of them with an air of the peasant art he so liked. There was a student at the school, a tall boy who had a weak back and needed to rest during lunch-hour. He kept a mattress rolled behind his workbench, and every day after lunch he'd spread this on the floor and take a nap. He had been working on an intricately carved lamp-stand for almost a month. Designed by the professor, it was all walnut and hard carving. One day just before lunchtime, the old man came along—and caught sight of the lamp-stand.

"Yes," he said, "it is not bad. But you have got to cut some more here, and then on that side, up there," he pointed. The wood-carver—his name was Eric—nodded sleepily, and the professor shuffled off, and out to a café for a leisurely lunch.

Later in the afternoon he was back. "There!" he cried excitedly, "what did I tell you? Now it is fine!"

Again Eric nodded. Satisfied, the old man went into the office. Eric winked at his neighbor, and kept on sharpening his tools. He had eaten, and slept, and felt good. The lamp was as it had been: Eric hadn't touched it since early that morning.

This is a rather personal sort of book—with whatever advantages and disadvantages such an attempt at communication involves. If I seem to presuppose that craft education, and the resulting efforts, does not often give us that side of a craft containing both knowledge *and* emotion—a hard-to-define element at once logical and intuitive —it is because I have met many students for whom this lack has been and still is all too real. Their education has led to Survival (a profession) rather than Self (a sense of fullfilment), to getting along rather than to happiness in a difficult medium.

So if I take the liberty of expressing my personal views and feelings, and sharing only first-hand experiences instead of undisputable facts, it is because I hope my probings will lead farther those who are also curious. Along the way I have tried to open little windows for myself—and for those who also want to look, and whose view will, I hope, be wider than mine has been.

I have not attempted to define, much less encompass, Cabinetmaking. Our craft extends beyond any man's knowledge or ambitions—that is its fascination. Those of us who want to do what we really care about need never be bored doing it. And if we are fortunate, we will share with others likewise inclined a certain feeling and warmtn. It encourages us towards learning, little discoveries, enjoyment. That is not a bad beginning.

James Krenov

INDEX